THE APHORISMS
OF THE
YOGA PHILOSOPHY,
OF
PATANJALI

THE APHORISMS
OF THE
YOGA PHILOSOPHY,
OF
PATANJALI

BY
BHOJA RAJA

GYAN

Published by

Gyan Publishing House
5, Ansari Road
Daryaganj, New Delhi-110002
Phone: 011-47034999, 9811692060
E-mail: books@gyanbooks.com

Distribution Network
gyanbooks.com
India, USA, Canada, UK, Australia, France

ISBN: 978-81-212-8120-1 (PB)
First Published, 1852

2nd Impression 2023

Printed at: Gyan Press, Delhi.

THE APHORISMS OF THE YOGA PHILOSOPHY OF PATANJALI
Author: BHOJA RAJA

THE APHORISMS

OF THE

YOGA PHILOSOPHY,

OF

PATANJALI

WITH

ILLUSTRATIVE EXTRACTS FROM THE COMMENTARY

BY

BHOJA RAJA.

PRINTED FOR THE USE OF THE BENARES COLLEGE
BY ORDER OF GOVT. N. W. P.

ALLAHABAD:
PRINTED AT THE PRESBYTERIAN MISSION PRESS.
Rev. L. G. HAY, *Sup't.*
1852.

PREFACE.

The great body of Hindú Philosophy is based upon six sets of very concise Aphorisms. Without a commentary the Aphorisms are scarcely intelligible, they being designed not so much to communicate the doctrine of the particular school, as to aid, by the briefest possible suggestions, the memory of him to whom the doctrine shall have been already communicated. To this end they are admirably adapted; and, this being their end, the obscurity, which must needs attach to them in the eyes of the uninstructed, is not chargeable upon them as a fault.

For various reasons it is desirable that there should be an accurate translation of the Aphorisms, with so much of gloss as may be required to render them intelligible. A class of pandits, in the Benares Sanskrit College, having been induced to learn English, it is contemplated that a version of the Aphorisms, brought out in successive portions, shall be submitted to the criticism of these men, and, through them, of other learned Bráhmans, so that any errors in the version may have the best chance of being discovered and rectified. The employment of such a version as a class-book is designed to subserve further the attempt to determine accurately the aspect of the philosophical terminology of the East as regards that of the West.

The translation of this first portion of the *Yoga* Aphorisms has been attended with peculiar difficulties, among which it may suffice here to mention that no pandit in these days professes to teach this system. That the version should, in its present state, be found faultless, is therefore very unlikely. These pages, now submitted to the criticism of the pandits who read English, are to be regarded as proof-sheets awaiting correction. They merely *moot* the subject, on which they invite discussion.

J. R. B.

Benares College,
8th Sept. 1851.

THE

YOGA APHORISMS

OF

PATANJALI.

INTRODUCTION.

a. Salutation to Gaṇeśa! May that union of the twin-persons of Siva and his spouse,—by the recollection of which one enjoys emancipation, hard as it is to attain,—produce for you all blessings!*

b. From such passages of scripture as this—viz.—"NÁCHIKETA having received this science [viz. the Vedánta] declared to him by Yama, and all the rules of the *yoga*, having arrived at the Supreme Soul, became passionless and immortal:—whosoever else also thus knows the Supreme Spirit, &c.,"—it is inferred that the rules of the *yoga* ought to be understood and practised by those who are desirous of emancipation. Therefore the venerable PATANJALI, being about to exhibit the rules of the *yoga*, in order to gain the attention of his disciples, states as follows what doctrine it is that is going to be entered upon.†

---

* श्री गणेशाय नमः। देहार्द्धयोगश्शिवयोस्स श्रेयांसि तनोतु वः। दुष्प्रापमपि यत्स्मृत्या जनः कैवल्यमश्नुते॥

† मृत्युप्रोक्तां नाचिकेतो ऽथ लब्ध्वा विद्यामेतां योगविधिञ्च कृत्स्नं ब्रह्मप्राप्तो विरजो ऽभूद्विमृत्युरन्यो ऽप्येवं यो वेदा

A

The subject proposed. अथातो योगानुशासनम्॥ १॥

Aph. 1.—Now, then, the exposition of Concentration [is to be made].

a. The expression 'Now, then,' intimates [that] a [distinct] topic [here commences]; and it serves as a benediction* [—the particle *atha* being regarded as an auspicious one].

b. The word *yoga*, from the root *yuj* 'to keep the mind fixed in abstract meditation,' means such a restraining of the exercise of the mind, or Concentration.†

c. An 'exposition' is that whereby something is expounded, or declared, through its characteristic marks, its nature, &c. An 'exposition *of* the *yoga*,'—[such is the meaning of the compound word] *yogánuśásana*. This [—viz. the expounding of the nature, &c., of Concentration—] is to be understood to be the topic even to the end of this Institute‡ [of PATANJALI's].

d. But what *is* Concentration *(yoga)*? To this he replies:§—

ध्य त्वमेवेत्यादिश्रुतिषु मुमुक्षूणां योगविधिरनुष्ठेयत्वेन ज्ञेय तयावगम्यतेऽतो योगविधिमुपदिदिक्षुर्भगवान् पतञ्जलिश्शिष्यावधानाय तच्छास्त्रारम्भं प्रतिजानीते ॥

* अथशब्दोऽधिकारद्योतको मङ्गलार्थश्च ॥

† युक्तिर्योगस्समाधानं । युज समाधौ ॥

‡ अनुशिष्यते व्याख्यायते लक्षणस्वरूपादिभिर्येन तदनुशासनं । योगस्यानुशासनं योगानुशासनम् । तदाशास्त्रपरिसमाप्तेरधिकृतं बोद्धव्यम् ॥

§ को योग इत्यत आह ॥

Concentration defined.

योगश्चित्तवृत्तिनिरोधः ॥ २ ॥

Aph. 2.—Concentration *(yoga)* is the hindering of the modifications of the thinking principle.

a. That is to say,—Concentration is the hindering, or the preventing, of the modifications—to be described hereafter [see §5] —of the Mind or internal organ [—to which modifications the internal organ is liable when allowed to come into contact with objects, as will be explained further on—]; and this 'hindering' is a super-sensual species of effort which is the cause of the destruction of these modifications.*

b. But then [a doubt may here occur]. It is a tenet [—see Nyáya Aphorisms No. 31—] both of the *Sánkhya* and the *Yoga* that the soul just consists of the knowledge which has as its objects the modifications [in question—the two being united] like fire and the wood [or fuel of the fire]:—on the destruction of the modifications, then, the Soul too should be annihilated, as the fire is in the absence of the fuel:—and therefore, at the time of Concentration, what is the soul concerned about? With reference to this he declares as follows:†—

Condition of the soul during concentration.

तदा द्रष्टुः स्वरूपे ऽवस्थानम् ॥ ३ ॥

Aph. 3.—Then [i. e. at the time of Concentration] it [the Soul] abides in the form of the spectator [without a spectacle.]

---

* चित्तस्यान्तःकरणस्य वक्ष्यमाणा या वृत्तयस्तासां निरोधो निवर्त्तनं योग इत्यर्थः। निवर्त्तनञ्चातीन्द्रियः प्रयत्नविशेषो वृत्तिविलयहेतुरिति ॥

† ननु वृत्तिविषयकबोधस्वरूप एव पुरुषः काष्ठाग्निवदिति

a. 'Then';—i. e. at that time.*

b. 'In the form of the spectator;'—i. e. of soul [—see *Tattwa-samása* §3 .—], in the form of Thought simply [without any object thought of]. 'Its state is' :—such is the force of the term *avasthána*† [rendered 'it abides,' &c.]

c. And so the definition [of Concentration] is this, that concentration is the hindering of the modifications of the internal organ [§2], which [prevention of its being modified] is the cause of the abiding in the form of soul simply.‡

d. What then is the form of this [Soul] when in a state other than that of Concentration? To this he replies :§—

Condition of the soul at other times.

वृत्तिसारूप्यमितरत्र ॥ ४ ॥

Aph. 4.—At other times [than that of Concentration] it [the soul] is in the same form as the modifications [of the internal organ—§ 2. *b*. and 5.] .

a. 'At other times;'—i. e. at another time than that of Concentration. The 'modifications' are those that are to be described

---

सांख्ययोगयोः सिद्धान्तो वृत्तिविलये पुरुषोऽपि नश्येत्काष्ठापायेऽग्निवत्ततश्च योगकाले कः पुरुषार्थ इत्याकाङ्क्षायामाह ॥

* तदा तस्मिन् काले ॥

† द्रष्टुः पुरुषस्य स्वरूपे। चिन्मात्रस्वरूपे। अवस्थानं। स्थितिर्भवति ॥

‡ तथाच द्रष्टुः स्वरूपावस्थितिहेतुश्चित्तवृत्तिनिरोधो योग इति लक्षणम् ॥

§ व्युत्थानदशायां तस्य किं स्वरूपमित्यत आह ॥

[see §5]. To be 'in the same form' as these—means to consist of these. The meaning [of the whole] is this, that when the internal organ [or Mind], through the senses, is affected [or modified] by the form of some object, the soul also [viewing the object through its organ the Mind] is as it were altered into that form, as the moon [reflected] in the moving ripples of the water, is like as if it were [itself] moving.*

b. Well, then:—it was stated that the modifications [of the internal organ] are to be hindered. Of how many kinds, then, are these [modifications], or what are they like? To this he replies:†—

The modifications of the thinking principle, how many and what like.

वृत्तयः पञ्चतय्यः क्लिष्टा अक्लिष्टाः ॥५॥

Aph. 5.—The Modifications [of the internal organ] are of five kinds, [and they are either] painful or not painful.

a. 'Modifications';—i. e. various altered states of the internal organ. 'Of five kinds,' or of five sorts. 'Painful';—i. e. invaded by vexations which will be defined in the sequel. 'Not painful';—i. e. the reverse thereof.‡

---

* इतरत्र योगादन्यस्मिन्काले । वृत्तयो वक्ष्यमाणलक्षणाः । ताभिस्सारूप्यं तद्रूपत्वं । अयमर्थश्चित्ते इन्द्रियद्वारा विषयाकारेण परिणते सति पुरुषस्तदाकार इव परिभाव्यते यथा जलतरङ्गेषु चलत्सु चन्द्रश्चलन्निव भवति तद्वदिति ॥

† ननु वृत्तयो निरोद्धव्या इत्युक्तं । ताः पुनः कियत्प्रकाराः कीदृश्यो वेत्याकाङ्क्षायामाह ॥

‡ वृत्तयश्चित्तपरिणामविशेषाः । पञ्चतय्यः पञ्चप्रकाराः ।

b. Which are those five Modifications? With reference to this, he states:*—

These Modifications specified.

प्रमाणविपर्ययविकल्पनिद्रास्मृतयः ॥ ६ ॥

Aph. 6.—[The modifications of the internal organ are] evidence [or right notion], misconception, fancy, sleep, and memory.

a. [All this is] clear.†

b. He defines these [modifications] in their order.‡

Right notions.

प्रत्यक्षानुमानागमाः प्रमाणानि ॥ ७ ॥

Aph. 7.—The evidences [§6.] are Perception, Inference, and Testimony.

a. Here [—it will be observed—] without stating the definition of the several kinds of evidence, this being so familiarly known, he has only divided them. [Lest, however, the reader should require the information, we may remark, in passing, that] the evidence called Perception is that modification of the internal organ which takes the form of assurance in respect of some object not previously apprehended. Inference is the modification of the internal organ produced from a correct notion of a general proposition, &c. [—respecting objects previously apprehended—

क्लिष्टाः क्लेशैर्वक्ष्यमाणलक्षणैराक्रान्ताः । अक्लिष्टास्तद्विपरीताः ॥

* काास्ताः पञ्च वृत्तय इत्याकाङ्क्षायामाह ॥

† स्पष्टम् ॥

‡ आसां क्रमेण लक्षणान्याह ॥

as explained in the works of the Nyáya]. And the evidence called Testimony is [what produces] that modification of the internal organ which arises from the words of one worthy* [to be received as an authority].

b. Having thus spoken of the modification of the internal organ which consists in evidence [—or, as we should rather say—which consists in the correct state of cognition resulting from good evidence—], he mentions that which is in the shape of misconception.†

Misconception what. विपर्ययो मिथ्याज्ञानमतद्रूपप्रतिष्ठम् ॥ ८ ॥

Aph. 8.—Misconception is incorrect notion, not staying in the [proper] form of that [in respect whereof the misconception is entertained].

a. [That is to say—] misconception is a notion arising, in respect of something that is *not* so and so, that it *is* so and so; as, in the case of mother o'pearl, the notion of silver. 'Not staying in the [proper] form of that';—that is to say, which does not abide in that form which is the form of that thing [in respect of which the notion is entertained],—which amounts to its not *revealing* the form [or real nature] which belongs to the thing.‡

---

* अत्रातिप्रसिद्धत्वात् प्रमाणानां लक्षणमनुक्त्वैव विभागः कृतः । तत्रानधिगतार्थनिश्चयरूपा चित्तवृत्तिः प्रत्यक्षं प्रमाणं । व्याप्त्यादिप्रमाजन्या वृत्तिरनुमानं । योग्यशब्दजन्यः वृत्तिश्च शब्दः प्रमाणमिति ॥

† एवं प्रमाणरूपां वृत्तिं व्याख्याय विपर्ययरूपामाह ॥

‡ अतथाभूतेऽर्थे तथोत्पद्यमानं ज्ञानं विपर्ययः । यथा

b. [To illustrate this language of our author, we may here state the theory of the Understanding which he adopts, as we find it laid down in the *Vedánta Paribháshá.* The internal organ is there compared to water, in respect of its readiness to adapt itself to the form of whatever mould it may enter. "As the water of a reservoir, having issued from an aperture, having entered, by a channel, the basins [or beds with raised edges formed in the fields that require irrigation—] becomes four-cornered or otherwise shaped just like these; so the manifesting internal organ [or Mind,] having gone, through the sight or other channel, to where there is an object, for instance a jar, becomes modified by the form of the jar or other object. It is this altered state [of the internal organ] that is called its modification."* This 'manifesting internal organ,' whilst it is regarded as moulding itself upon the object, is regarded as at the same time manifesting it—or revealing it as a mirror does. To a considerable extent this theory of the Understanding is analogous to the theory of vision entertained by those who regard the retina as reflecting to the intelligent principle those visible forms of which the retina itself is uncognisant; whilst the intelligent principle itself is cognisant of things visible only inasmuch as they are reflected to it by the retina. The 'modifications' are akin to Locke's 'ideas'].

शुक्तिकायां रजतज्ञानं। अतद्रूपप्रतिष्ठमिति। तस्यार्थस्य यद्रूपं न तस्मिन् रूपे प्रतिष्ठते। तस्यार्थस्य यद्रूपं न तत्प्रतिभासयतीति यावत्॥

* यथा तडागोदकं छिद्रान्निर्गत्य कुल्यात्मना केदारान् प्रविश्य तद्वदेव चतुष्कोणाद्याकारं भवति तथा तैजसमन्तःकरणमपि चक्षुरादिद्वारा घटादिविषयदेशं गत्वा घटादिविषयाकारेण परिणमते। स एव परिणामो वृत्तिरित्युच्यते॥ वेद॰ परि॰॥

c. Doubt also—for example whether the object be a man or a post—is incorrect notion [§ 8], inasmuch as the real nature of the object is not thereby revealed.*

d. In order to declare what modification [of the internal organ] is fancy—he says as follows :—†

Fanciful notions what. शब्दज्ञानानुपाती वस्तुशून्यो विकल्पः ॥९॥

Aph. 9.—A fancy is [a notion] devoid of a thing [in reality corresponding thereto], following upon knowledge [conveyed] by words.

a. 'Knowledge produced [or conveyed] by words :'—[such is the sense of the compound] *śabda-jnána.* 'That, the habit whereof is to follow this [verbal information],' is what is so named [viz. fancy]. The meaning is—that a fancy is a conception, without a thing‡ [corresponding to it].

b. Examples of this are such notions as 'The head of *Ráhu,*' and 'The soul's Thinking,'—and 'Something like the horns of a a hare,' &c. Even after [discovering] the absurdity [involved in such notions], people yet deal with verbal knowledge [as if it were strictly receivable] in such senses, [—and it depends upon

---

* संशयोऽप्यतद्रूपप्रतिष्ठत्वान्मिथ्याज्ञानं यथा स्थाणुर्वा पुरुषो वेति ॥

† विकल्पवृत्तिं व्याख्यातुमाह ।

‡ शब्दजनितं ज्ञानं शब्दज्ञानं । तदनुपतितुं शीलं यस्य स तथोक्तः । वस्तुशून्यः प्रत्ययो विकल्प इत्यर्थः ।

B

circumstances whether any serious error is to result from this or not.]*

c. [As a hare has no horn, the notion of a hare's horn is a fanciful one, 'devoid of a thing *in rerum naturâ* corresponding to the notion.' A person hearing the expression 'The head of *Ráhu*' naturally proceeds to fancy that there is some *Ráhu* to whom this head belongs;—but *Ráhu* is *all* head—being a bodiless monster who is held to cause eclipses by swallowing the sun and moon, which emerge from obscuration when they come to the end of his dissevered gullet. The notion, therefore, raised by the expression 'The head of *Ráhu*,' that there is any more of him besides the head, is a fancy—equally with that of the hare's horn—'devoid of a thing corresponding to the notion.' So again, a person hearing the expression 'The soul's Thinking,' naturally proceeds to fancy that there is some Soul to whom this Thinking belongs,—whereas the Soul is nothing besides the Thinking. Although, according to the commentator, such expressions are liable to suggest fancies that have nothing in reality corresponding to them, yet the employment of the expressions does not necessarily mislead if we carefully bear in mind what is the real state of the case. Much on the same principle people in Europe continue to speak of the sun's rising and setting, though, holding the heliocentric theory, they do not really fancy that the sun either rises or sets].

d. In order to declare what is sleep, he says†—

---

* अस्योदाहरणानि। राहोश्शिरः। पुरुषस्य चैतन्यम्। शशशृङ्गतुल्यमित्यादिज्ञानानि। बाधोत्तरमप्येतादृशज्ञाने शब्दज्ञानरूपो व्यवहारः क्रियत इति।

† निद्रां व्याख्यातुमाह।

Definition of sound sleep.

अभावप्रत्ययालम्बना वृत्तिर्निद्रा ॥ १० ॥

Aph. 10.—Sleep is that modification [of the internal organ] which depends on the conception of nothing.

a. Of what modification [of the internal organ] the ground is the conception of nothing, this is what is so called* [—viz. sleep].

b. This may be [also] stated as follows :—Sleep is that modification [of the internal organ] which takes place on the quitting of all objects, through [the quality of] Darkness's getting everywhere the upper hand† [—to the exclusion of the other two qualities, which,—see Lecture on the Sánkhya § 96,—are held to be constituents of the phenomenal universe].

c. And the fact that this [dreamless sleep] *is* a modification [of the internal organ, and not a mere blank,] is [proved] by our seeing that one recollects [on arising from profound and dreamless sleep] that 'I slept pleasantly;'—and there could not be a *recollection* if there had not been a state of consciousness‡ [to furnish the matter of the recollection. Conf. Lecture on the Vedánta § 33].

d. In order to describe memory, he says§—

---

* अभावप्रत्यय आलम्बनं यस्या वृत्तेस्सा तथोक्ता ॥

† एतदुक्तं भवति। या सन्ततमुद्रिक्तत्वात्तमसः समस्त विषयपरित्यागेन प्रवर्त्तते वृत्तिस्सा निद्रेति ॥

‡ अस्याश्च सुखमहमस्वाप्समिति स्मृतिदर्शनात् स्मृतेश्चानुभवव्यतिरेकेणानुपपत्तेर्वृत्तित्वम् ॥

§ स्मृतिं व्याख्यातुमाह ॥

Memory defined.

अनुभूतविषयासम्प्रमोषः स्मृतिः ॥ ११ ॥

Aph. 11.—Memory is the not letting go of an object that one has been aware of.

a. [That is to say]—memory [or recollection] is the not letting go—or, by means of the self-reproductive quality [of the Soul —see *Tarka Sangraha* p 55]—the arising, in the understanding, of that which has been cognised through evidence* [of the senses, for example;—see § 7].

Waking, sleeping, and dreaming.

b. Of these [modifications of the internal organ, the three following, viz.] right notion [§ 7. *a.*] misconception [§ 8.] and fancy [§ 9.] are *waking* states. When just these [impressions—in the absence of the objects or of what gave rise to them] are sensible, through the force [or vividness] of the impression, then there is *dream.* But [dreamless] sleep [§ 10] is without any object cognised. And Recollection may take its rise either in a right notion, in a misconception, in a fancy, or in [dreamless] sleep† [—see § 10. *c.*]

c. Having thus described the modifications [of the internal organ], in order to explain the prevention of these [§ 2. *a.*], with the means thereof, he says‡—

---

* प्रमाणेनानुभूतस्य यो ऽयमसम्प्रमोषः संस्कारद्वारेण बुद्धावारोहः सा स्मृतिः ॥

† तत्र प्रमाणविपर्य्ययविकल्पा जाग्रदवस्थाः । त एव यदा- नुभवबलात्प्रत्यक्षायमाणास्तदा स्वप्नः । निद्रात्वसंवेद्यमान- विषया । स्मृतिश्च प्रमाणविपर्य्ययविकल्पनिद्रानिमित्ता ॥

‡ एवं वृत्तीर्व्याख्याय सोपायं निरोधं व्याख्यातुमाह ॥

अभ्यासवैराग्याभ्यां तन्निरोधः ॥ १२ ॥

Asceticism and mortification the means of repelling the transient.

Aph. 12. The hindering of these [modifications of the internal organ —§ 2—is to be effected] by means of exercise and dispassion.

a. 'Exercise and dispassion' will be defined [in § 13 and 15]. By these [viz. exercise and dispassion], the repelling of those modifications of the internal organ which [modifications, at different times] have the form of revealing, energising, and obstructing, —*this* is the 'hindering'—[which is to be striven after, and which is tantamount to] the resting [of these modifications], in a potential shape, in their cause, viz: in the internal organ* [without taking an actual shape as products of the internal organ modified.]

b. Of the two [viz. exercise and dispassion, §12,] it is from 'dispassion,' which originates in our discerning the perniciousness of the objective, that aversion thereto arises. And, by 'exercise,' confirmed steadfastness [in the indifference towards all objects] is produced. So, by these two, the internal organ is hindered from undergoing modification.†

---

* अभ्यासवैराग्ये वक्ष्यमाणलक्षणे । ताभ्यां तासां प्रकाशप्रवृत्तिनियमरूपाणां चित्तवृत्तीनां यत्प्रतिहननं स निरोधः । स्वकारण एव चित्ते शक्तिरूपतयावस्थानम् ॥

† तत्र विषयदोषदर्शनजेन वैराग्येण तद्वैमुख्यमुत्पाद्यते । अभ्यासेनच दृढं स्थैर्यमुत्पाद्यते । इत्याभ्यां भवति चित्तवृत्तिनिरोधः ॥

d. In order to describe 'exercise' [§12] he says.*—

Ascetic effort what. तत्र स्थितौ यत्नोऽभ्यासः ॥ १३ ॥

Aph. 13.—'Exercise' is the [repeated] effort that it [—viz. the internal organ—] shall remain in its [unmodified] state.

a. The condition of the internal organ, when free from modification, existing only in its own [unmodified] form, is what we mean by its [unmodified] state. And what we mean by 'exercise' is the effort, or endeavour, again and again to reduce the internal organ to such a condition† [of freedom from modification].

b. He next mentions a special character of this same‡ [exercise, or persevering effort].

स तु दीर्घकालनैरन्तर्यसत्कारसेवितो दृढभूमिः ॥ १४ ॥

Aph. 14.—But this [exercise—§13--] is a firm position observed out of regard [for the end in view, and perseveringly adhered to] for a long time unintermittingly.

a. That is to say :—it [—exercise—] is a firm ground [or state of steadfastness],—to be firm [we may remark in passing] is to be steadfast,—this [state of steadfastness] being assiduously attend-

---

* अभ्यासं व्याख्यातुमाह ॥

† वृत्तिरहितस्य चित्तस्य स्वरूपनिष्ठः परिणामः स्थितिः। तस्याञ्च यत्न उत्साहः पुनः पुनस्तथात्वेन चेतसि विनिवेशनमभ्यास इत्युच्यते ॥

‡ तस्यैव विशेषमाह ॥

ed to, during a long time unintermittingly, out of the excess of regard* [which one entertains for the end to be gained].

b. He now mentions the definition of 'dispassion'† [§12].

Dispassion defined. दृष्टानुश्रविकविषयवितृष्णस्य वशीकारसंज्ञा वैराग्यम् ॥ १५ ॥

Aph. 15. Dispassion is the consciousness of having overcome [one's desires,—this consciousness being that] of him who thirsts after neither the objects that are seen [on earth] nor those that are heard of [in scripture].

a. Object is of two kinds—'seen' *(dṛishṭa)* and 'heard of' *(ánuśravika)*. One 'seen' is one apprehended here [on earth]—such as a Sound [or other object of sense]. One 'heard of' means one in the world of the gods or elsewhere [where it cannot be seen by us]. The *Veda* is called *anuśrava* because it is [not first *read* by the young student, but is] listened to *(śrúyate)* from the mouth of the preceptor [—and heard *after*, or consequently on, the teacher's utterance,—as the prefix *anu* implies]. What [object] comes [to our knowledge] therefrom [i. e. from the Veda] is what we mean by one 'heard of'‡ *(ánuśravika)*.

b. What is called 'dispassion' is the reflection "These [objects —whether of this world or of the one beyond—§15. *a.*—] are *my*

---

* बहुकालं नैरन्तर्येणादरातिशयेन सेव्यमानो दृढभूमिः स्थिरो भवति दार्ढ्याय भवतीत्यर्थः ॥

† वैराग्यस्य लक्षणमाह ॥

‡ द्विविधो विषयो दृष्ट आनुश्रविकश्च । दृष्ट इहैवोपलभ्यमानशब्दादिः । देवलोकादावानुश्रविकः । अनुश्रूयते गुरुमुखादित्यनुश्रवो वेदस्तत आगत आनुश्रविकः ॥

subjects; I am not *their* slave,"—this 'consciousness of having overcome' entertained by h m who, from discerning the insipidity of the results of both of those [classes of objects] has dismissed all eagerness about them.*

c. He next mentions a peculiar aspect of this same† [i. e. of 'dispassion.']

Dispassion carried the length of indifference to all objects.

तत्परं पुरुषख्यातेर्गुणवैतृष्ण्यम् ॥ १६ ॥

Aph. 16.—This [viz. 'dispassion,'] carried to the utmost is indifference regarding the 'qualities' [i. e. everything else than Soul], and this indifference arises from a knowledge of Soul [as distinguished from the 'qualities.' See Lecture on the *Sánkhya* §49].

a. 'This:'—i. e. 'dispassion,' 'carried to the utmost:'—i. e. elevated [to its utmost]. The first [degree of 'dispassion,'—see §15—] has regard to [ordinary] *objects*;—but the second [§16], has regard to the 'qualities' [from which, according to the Sánkhya, ordinary objects arise]. This arises only from familiarity with the distinction between the 'qualities' and Soul [—or the objective and subjective]. From its extreme conduciveness to abstract meditation‡ [it ranks above the dispassion which has regard only to the grosser objects].

---

* तयोर्द्वयोरपि परिणामविरसत्वदर्शनाद्विगतगर्द्धस्य या वशीकारसंज्ञा ममैत वशाः नाहमेतेषां वश इति योऽयं विमर्शस्तद्वैराग्यमुच्यते ॥

† तस्यैव विशेषमाह ॥

‡ तद्वैराग्यं। परमुत्कृष्टं। प्रथमं वैराग्यं विषयविषयं द्वितीयन्तु गुणविषयमुत्पन्नगुणपुरुषविवेकख्यातेरेव भवति निरोधसमाधेरत्यन्तानुकूलत्वात् ॥

b. Having thus stated the nature of concentration (*Yoga*), he [next] mentions the difference between the nature of [meditation, which is of two kinds—viz.] that 'in which there is distinct recognition,' *(samprajnáta)* and that 'in which distinct recognition is lost,'* *(a-samprajnáta).*

वितर्कविचारानन्दास्मितानुगमात्सम्प्रज्ञातः ॥ १७ ॥

Meditation, with an object.

Aph. 17.—[Meditation—of the kind called] that 'in which there is distinct recognition' [arises, in its fourfold shape,] from the attendance of (1) 'argumentation' *(vitarka),* (2) 'deliberation' *(vichára),* (3) 'beatitude' *(ánanda),* and (4) 'egotism' *(asmitá).*

a. The word 'Meditation' is required to supply the ellipsis in the aphorism.†

b. Meditation 'in which there is distinct recognition' *(samprajnáta)* is a kind of 'pondering' *(bhávaná)* whereby the nature of that which is to be pondered is known thoroughly and well—apart from either doubt or error. This meditation 'in which there is distinct recognition' excludes every modification of the mind [or every idea—see §8. *b*] other than what is to be pondered:—it is, in short, meditation with its *seed*‡ [i. e. with the

* एवं योगस्य स्वरूपमुक्त्वा सम्प्रज्ञातासम्प्रज्ञातस्वरूपभेदमाह ॥

† समाधिरिति शेषः ।

‡ सम्यक् संशयविपर्ययरहितत्वेन प्रज्ञायते प्रकर्षेण ज्ञायते भाव्यस्वरूपं येन स सम्प्रज्ञातः समाधिर्भावनाविशेषः। ध्येयातिरिक्तसकलवृत्तिनिरोधस्सम्प्रज्ञातस्सबीजसमाधिरिति यावत् ॥

object, in the effort to apprehend which exclusively the meditation originates].

c. This [meditation 'in which there is distinct recognition'—§ 17—], through its division into the 'argumentative' &c., is of four kinds, viz. (1) the 'argumentative,' (2) the 'deliberative,' (3) the 'beatific,' and (4) the 'egotistical.'*

d. As for 'Pondering' [§17. *b.*], this means the taking into the mind again and again, to the exclusion of all other objects, that which is to be pondered. And that which is [a suitable object] to be pondered is of two kinds, being either the Lord (*íś-wara*) or the twenty-five principles [—see *Tattwa-samása* §37—]. These [twenty-five principles] also are of two kinds, through their distinction as senseless and not senseless. Twenty-four [of the principles, including Earth, &c.], are senseless:—that which is not senseless is Soul.†

e. Among these [objects suitable for being pondered—§17 *d.*—] when, having taken as the object the Senses and the Elements which are gross [in comparison with the Subtile Elements next to be spoken of], pondering is engaged in, in the shape of the investigation as to which is antecedent and which is consequent [—i. e. whether the Senses generate the Elements or the

* स सवितर्कादिभेदाच्चतुर्विधः सवितर्कस्सविचारस्सानन्दस्सास्मितश्च ।

† भावना तावत् । भाव्यस्य विषयान्तरपरिहारेण चेतसि पुनः पुनर्निवेशनं । भाव्यञ्च द्विधा ईश्वरस्तत्त्वानिच पञ्चविंशतिः । तान्यपि द्विविधानि जडाजडभेदात् । जडानि चतुर्विंशतिरजडः पुरुषः ।

Elements generate the senses—] then the Meditation is [technically said to be] 'argumentative' *(savitarka)*.*

f. **When, having taken as the object something subtile, as the Subtile Elements and the Internal Organ, pondering is engaged in, in so far as regards the *where* and the *when* thereof,—then it [—the pondering—] is [technically said to be] 'deliberative' *(savichára)*.†**

g. But when the 'pure element' (*sattwa*—see *Sánkhya Lecture* §50) of the Internal Organ, commingled with somewhat of [the two other elements,—viz.] 'passion' and 'darkness' [—*Sánkhya Lecture* §51 and 52], is pondered, then the meditation is [technically termed] 'beatific' (*sánanda*—§17 *c.*), because the 'pure element' then pondered, which consists in the manifestation of joy [*Sánkhya Lecture* §50], is predominant—inasmuch as the intellectual faculty is then [—i. e. in this particular case of pondering—] a secondary matter.‡

h. After that [pondering of the 'pure element' commingled with the two others—§ 17. *g.*—], the meditation which is engaged in, having, as that on which it rests, the clear 'pure element' unaffected by even a little of 'passion' or 'darkness,' is called 'egotistical' meditation [§17. *c.*], because, here, [personal] ex-

---

* तत्र यदा महाभूतेन्द्रियाणि स्थूलानि विषयत्वेनादाय पूर्वापरानुसन्धानेन भावना प्रवर्त्तते तदा सवितर्कः समाधिः॥

† तन्मात्रान्तःकरणलक्षणं सूक्ष्मं विषयमालम्ब्य तस्य देशकालधर्मावच्छेदेन यदा भावना प्रवर्त्तते तदा सविचारः।

‡ यदा तु रजस्तमोलेशानुविद्धमन्तःकरणसत्त्वं भाव्यते तदा गुणभावाच्चिच्छक्तेः सुखप्रकाशमयस्य सत्त्वस्य भाव्यमानस्योद्रेकात्सानन्दः समाधिर्भवति॥

istence only remains, since the intellectual faculty becomes now predominent inasmuch as the 'pure element' which is to be apprehended [as the object of the meditation] is here disregarded* [as the mere stepping stone to higher things].

i. Among these [four kinds of 'meditation, where there is distinct recognition' of an object,—§ 17. *c.*], the first, the 'argumentative' meditation [§ 17. *e.*] includes all [that belongs to] the four. The second, the 'deliberative,' leaves out the 'argumentation' [of the preceding]:—the third, the 'beatific,' leaves out the deliberation [of the second]:—the fourth, consisting in mere self-consciousness, leaves out that [beatitude which belongs to the third]:—and all these [four] are meditations with something to rest upon† [as the object pondered;—the soul of the ascetic, like the body of the young swimmer, requiring supports to begin with, which are successively laid aside as power and confidence are gained by practice].

j. He next tells what is meant by that [meditation] 'in which distinct recognition is lost'‡ [§ 16. *b.*—the practised ascetic having parted with every vestige of object, as the practised swimmer with his last cork or bladder].

---

* ततः परं रजस्तमोलेशानभिभूतं शुद्धं सत्त्वमालम्बनीकृत्य या प्रवर्त्तते भावना तस्यां ग्राह्यस्य सत्त्वस्य न्यग्भावात् चिच्छक्तेरुद्रेकात्सत्तामात्रावशेषत्वेन समाधिः सास्मित इत्युच्यते।

† तत्र प्रथमश्चतुष्टयानुगतः समाधिः सवितर्कः। द्वितीयो वितर्कविकलः सविचारः। तृतीयो विचारविकलः सानन्दः। चतुर्थस्तद्विकलोऽस्मितामात्र इति सर्व एते सालम्बनाः समाधय इति॥

‡ असम्प्रज्ञातमाह॥

विरामप्रत्ययाभ्यासपूर्व्वः संस्कारशेषो ऽन्यः ॥ १८ ॥

Meditation without an object. *Aph.* 18.—The one [kind of meditation just described] is preceded by the exercise of thought in the shape of repose ;—the other [—independent of any fresh antecedent—] is in the shape of the self-reproduction [of thought, after the departure of all objects].

a. By 'repose' *(viráma)* we mean that whereby one is rested,—the abandonment of all anxiety about argumentation, &c. [§ 17.]. Well—'thought' in the shape of this 'repose' is what we mean by the compound expression *viráma-pratyaya* ;—and what we mean by the 'exercise' *(abhyása)* of this, is the reiteratedly dwelling mentally thereon, and constantly rejecting with a negative [as a delusion and an unreality] whatever 'modification' [or idea,—see § 5.—] springs up there [to interfere with it] ;—such is 'the exercise of thought in the shape of repose.' This [as remarked in the first half of the aphorism] produces meditation 'in which there is distinct recognition'* [§17 :—and we have now to consider that kind of meditation which differs from this].

b The other [kind of meditation] has nothing left but the self-reproduction of thought. It is different from that [above described] ; that is to say, it is [as contra-distinguished from meditation 'in which there is distinct recognition,'] that 'in which distinct recognition is lost.' Here there is nothing to be thought of or accurately apprehended [—as it was necessary that there should be in the former process—] ;—it is meditation *without* a

* विरम्यते अनेनेति विरामः। वितर्कादिचिन्तापरित्यागः। विरामश्चासौ प्रत्ययश्च विरामप्रत्ययः। तस्याभ्यासः पौनःपुन्येन चेतसि निवेशनं तत्र याकाचिद्वृत्तिरुल्लसति तस्यां नेति नेतीति नैरन्तर्य्येण पर्युदसनं विरामप्रत्ययाभ्यासः। तत्पूर्वकस्सम्प्रज्ञातसमाधिः।

seed* [—i. e. without any object—see §17 *b.*—in any effort to confine one's self to the apprehension of which the meditation has been entered upon].

c. Well, having thus stated the [two] distinctions [§18] in the nature of Concentration [§2], and having compendiously mentioned its methods, the author proceeds to speak of these methods more fully, first premising some account of the spurious semblance of concentration.†

भवप्रत्ययो विदेहप्रकृतिलयानाम् ॥ १९ ॥

Spurious semblances of abstract Meditation.

Aph. 19.—Of [the meditative state attained to by the two classes of aspirants, technically called] 'the unembodied and resolved into Nature,' *the world* is the cause.

a. By 'the unembodied and resolved into Nature' we mean to speak of [those technically called] 'the unembodied' [as one set], and 'the resolved into Nature' [as another set]. Of these the Meditation is caused by *the world*,—that is to say, it is such that the cause, or instrumental agency on which it depends, is the world—the creation—[—the phenomenal—beyond which the vision of these extends not to the discrimination of pure Spirit, and the uncreated energy Nature].‡

---

* संस्कारशेषोऽन्यः तद्विलक्षणः। असम्प्रज्ञात इत्यर्थः। न त्वत्र किञ्चिद्वेद्यं सम्प्रज्ञायत इत्यसम्प्रज्ञातो निर्बीजसमाधिः॥

† तदेवं योगस्य स्वरूपभेदं संक्षेपेणोपायञ्चाभिधाय विस्तरेणोपायं योगाभासप्रदर्शनपूर्वकं वक्तुमुपक्रमते।

‡ विदेहाश्च प्रकृतिलयाश्च विदेहप्रकृतिलयाः। तेषां समाधिर्भवप्रत्ययः भवः संसार एव प्रत्ययः कारणं यस्य तादृशो भवतीत्यर्थः।

b. The meaning is this—that, only while the world is manifest, are these men participators in such [inadequate] meditation [as we have described]. And this is a mere false semblance of meditation, because these do not discern the ultimate Reality. Hence, by him who desires emancipation, effort is to be made for [attaining to] the knowledge of the ultimate Reality, and for pondering *that** [instead of the lower things pondered by those of narrower ken, whose vision cannot pierce the phenomenal, and discriminate the spectator Soul, and the *natura naturans*].

c. And, of the persons spoken of in the aphorism, those who, having their energies directed to 'beatific' meditation [§17. *g.*], do not discern any other Reality, in the shape of Nature or Soul, these are they who are meant by the term the 'unembodied' *(videha)*, because their body and their self-consciousness are departed [—but they are not *further* advanced towards emancipation]. And those who [going just one step further] are content with the 'egotistic' meditation [§17. *h.*] but do not discern the Supreme Soul, and whose intellect has been resolved into [the *natura naturans* which is] its cause, these are they who are called the 'resolved into nature'† *(prakritilaya)*—[See *Sánkhya Lecture*, §15 and 54].

---

* अयमर्थः। आविर्भूतमात्र एव संसारे तथाविधसमाधिभाजो भवन्ति। तेषां परतत्त्वादर्शनात् योगाभासोऽयं। अतः परतत्त्वज्ञाने तद्भावनायाञ्च मुक्तिकामेन यत्नो विधेय इति।

† अत्रच ये सानन्दसमाधौ बद्धधृतयस्तत्त्वान्तरं प्रधानपुरुषरूपं न पश्यन्ति ते विगतदेहाहङ्कारत्वाद्विदेहशब्दवाच्याः। येच सास्मितसमाधौ कृतपरितोषाः परं परमात्मानं न पश्यन्ति येषाञ्च चेतस्स्वकारणे लयमुपगतं ते प्रकृतिलया इत्युच्यन्ते॥

d. But of others than those* [whose inadequate style of meditation has been stated in aphorism 19, the meditation is as stated in the aphorism here following].

श्रद्धावीर्यस्मृतिसमाधिप्रज्ञापूर्वक इतरेषाम् ॥ २० ॥

The genuine order of abstract Meditation.

Aph. 20.—[In the practice] of others, this [Meditation] is preceded by Faith, Energy, Memory, Meditation, and Discernment.

a. "Of others"—i. e. of *Yogís* other than [those called] the 'unembodied' [§ 19. *c.*] and the 'resolved into nature'† [§ 19. *c.*].

b. "Preceded by Faith, &c." To complete the sense, we must supply the word 'Meditation.' 'Preceded by Faith, &c.,'—that is to say—the means antecedent [and conducive] to which are Faith, &c. And these, 'Faith, &c.,' acting in the relation of means to an end, constitute the means [or appliances] for Meditation 'in which there is distinct recognition'‡ [—§ 17.].

Faith defined.

c. Among these [antecedents enumerated in the Aphorism], 'Faith' *(śraddhá)* means a mental approval of Concentration§ [as a worthy and possible aim].

Energy.

d. 'Energy' *(vírya)* means perseverance.||

---

* तदन्येषान्तु ॥

† इतरेषां । विदेहप्रकृतिलयव्यतिरिक्तानां योगिनां ॥

‡ श्रद्धादिपूर्वकः । श्रद्धादयः पूर्वं उपाया यस्य स श्रद्धादिपूर्वकस्समाधिरिति शेषः । तेच श्रद्धादय उपायोपेयभावेन प्रवर्त्तमानाः सम्प्रज्ञातस्य समाधेरुपायतां प्रतिपद्यन्ते ।

§ तत्र श्रद्धा योगविषये चेतसः प्रसादः ।

|| वीर्यमुत्साहः ।

Memory.

e. 'Memory' [or 'Recollection'—*smriti*] has already been explained,* [—see § 11].

Meditation.

f. 'Meditation' *(samádhi)* means intentness on a single point.†

Discernment.

g. 'Discernment' *(prajná)* means thorough discrimination of that which is to be known.‡

Reason for this order of statement.

h. Among these [antecedents,—to account for the order of statement adopted in the aphorism, we may remark, that]—of him who has 'Faith' there arises 'Energy,'—he becomes persevering in meditation;—and to one thus persevering the 'Memory' of past subjects springs up; and his mind becomes absorbed in 'Meditation' in consequence of the recollection thereof; and he whose mind is absorbed in meditation arrives at a thorough 'Discernment' of the matter pondered.§

i. Such are [according to those whose practice is recorded in §20.] the means of that Meditation 'in which there is distinct recognition' [§ 17.]. The [still higher step—the] Meditation 'in which distinct recognition is lost' [§ 18.] is arrived at through diligent practice [§ 13.] of this ['in which there *is* distinct recog-

---

* स्मृतिर्व्याख्याता।

† समाधिरेकाग्रता।

‡ प्रज्ञा ज्ञातव्यप्रविवेकः।

§ तत्र श्रद्धावतो वीर्यं जायते योगविषये उत्साहवान् भवति सोत्साहस्य च पाश्चात्यासु भूमिषु स्मृतिरुपजायते तत्स्मरणाच्चेतस्समाधीयते समाहितचित्तस्य भाव्यं सम्यग्विजानाति।

D

nition' of some object pondered], and through extreme 'Dispassion'* [§ 16].

j. He next mentions the subdivisions of *Yogis*, adopting the abovementioned means, according to the difference of method adopted by them.†

तीव्रसंवेगानामासन्नः ॥ २१ ॥

Ascetics divisible according to their method of procedure.

Aph. 21.—[The attainment of the state of abstract Meditation is] speedy in the case of the hotly impetuous.

a. To complete the aphorism, the words 'The attainment of the state of abstract Meditation' require to be supplied.‡

b. By 'impetuosity' *(samvega)* is meant a more energetic self-reproducing impulse, which is a cause of action. Those persons in whose 'transcendent' methods [§ 22.] this [impetuosity] is violent, are close upon the attainment of abstract meditation and the fruits of meditation;—that is to say, this is, in their case, rapidly brought about.§

---

* त एते सम्प्रज्ञातसमाधेरुपायाः। तस्याभ्यासात्पराच्च वैराग्याद्भवत्यसम्प्रज्ञातः ॥

† उक्तोपायवतां योगिनामुपायभेदाद्भेदानाह ॥

‡ समाधिलाभ इति शेषः।

§ संवेगः क्रियाहेतुर्दृढतरसंस्कारः स तीव्रो येषामधिमात्रोपायानां तेषामासन्नस्समाधिलाभस्समाधिफलञ्चासन्नं भवति शीघ्रमेव निष्पद्यत इत्यर्थः ॥

c. *Who* are those 'hotly impetuous' [§ 21]? To this he replies.*

मृदुमध्याधिमात्रत्वात्ततोऽपि विशेषः ॥ २२ ॥

Aph. 22.—Through the 'mild,' the 'medium,' and the 'transcendent' [nature of the methods adopted] there is thence also a distinction [among the ascetics who adopt the methods].

a. Through the diversity of these various methods, viz. the 'mild' &c., there is a distinction of those who employ the methods. The divisions of method are the 'mild' *(mridu)*, the 'medium' *(madhya)*, and the 'transcendent' *(adhimátra)*. These are severally threefold from their being severally subdivided into the 'mildly impetuous,' the 'middlingly impetuous,' and the 'transcendently impetuous.'

The nine divisions of ascetics.

And in accordance with this division there are nine classes of followers of the *Yoga*. Thus—there is the 'mild method'—[the follower of which may be] the 'mildly impetuous,' the 'middlingly impetuous,' or the 'transcendently impetuous.' Then there is the 'medium method'—[the follower of which may be] the 'mildly impetuous,' the 'middlingly impetuous,' or the 'transcendently impetuous.' And there is the 'transcendent method'—[the follower of which may be] the 'mildly impetuous,' the 'middlingly impetuous,' or the 'transcendently impetuous'. And great endeavours ought to be made after the 'transcendent method' and after warm impetuosity [in following out the same]. So much for the declaration of the distinctions† [among the followers of the *Yoga*].

---

* के ते तीव्रसंवेगा इत्यत आह ॥

† तेभ्य उपायेभ्यो मृद्वादिभेदभिन्नेभ्य उपायवतां विशेषो भवति। मृदुर्मध्योऽधिमात्र इत्युपायभेदाः। ते प्रत्येकं मृदु-

b. By 'mildness' [as we learn from Bhávágaṇeśa] is here meant 'smallness'. The meaning of 'middlingness' is the familiar one. By 'transcendentness' is meant the exceeding of all measure,—excessiveness, in short*.

c. Now he mentions a method which differs from these methods in being an easy one.†

ईश्वरप्रणिधानाद्वा ॥ २३ ॥

The devotional method. *Aph.* 23—Or by profound devotedness towards the Lord, [the ascetic may attain to the state of abstract Meditation].

a. By "the Lord" (*íśwara*) we mean what will be defined [in §24]. By "profound devotedness" towards Him, we mean a kind of devoted attachment, a peculiar serving of Him, the consigning of all one's actions to Him. The person [under the influence we speak of] desiring no fruit [of his actions] in the shape of enjoyment of sense-objects, or the like, makes over all his ac-

---

संवेगमध्यसंवेगतीव्रसंवेगभेदात्त्रिविधाः। तद्भेदेनच नव योगिनो भवन्ति। मृदूपायः। मृदुसंवेगो मध्यसंवेगः तीव्रसंवेगश्च। मध्योपायः। मृदुसंवेगो मध्यसंवेगः तीव्रसंवेगश्च। अधिमात्रोपायः। मृदुसंवेगो मध्यसंवेगः तीव्रसंवेगश्च। अधिमात्रोपाये तीव्रेच संवेगे महान् यत्नः कर्त्तव्य इति भेदोपदेशः॥

* मृदुत्वमल्पता। मध्यत्वं प्रसिद्धम्। अधिमात्रत्वमतिप्रमाणत्वमतिशयितत्वमिति यावत्॥ इति भावागणेशः॥

† इदानीमेतदुपायविलक्षणं सुगममुपायान्तरमाह॥

tions to Him, the pre-eminent guide. This 'profound devotedness' is a pre eminent means of abstract Meditation and of the attainment of its fruits.*

The devotional method has reference to the 'Lord.'

b. It has been just stated that abstract Meditation may be attained through profound devotedness towards *the Lord.* With reference to this, he now proceeds to declare, in order, the nature, [§24] the proofs [§25], the pre-eminence [§26], and the name [§27], of the Lord, the order of His worship [§28], and the fruit thereof† [§29].

क्लेशकर्मविपाकाशयैरपरामृष्टपुरुषविशेष ईश्वरः ॥ २४ ॥

The term 'Lord' defined.

Aph. 24.—The Lord is a particular Spirit *(purusha)* untouched by troubles, works, fruits, or deserts.

a. 'Troubles'—i. e. things that distress,—such as ignorance &c.. which will be spoken of [in the 2nd section]. 'Works'—i. e. [actions involving] merit or demerit. 'Fruits'—i. e. what ripen out of works, as birth, life, or whatever is experienced [by mortals as the consequences of their actions]. By 'deserts' are

---

* ईश्वरो वक्ष्यमाणलक्षणः। प्रणिधानं तत्र भक्तिविशेषो विशिष्टमुपासनं सर्वक्रियाणामपि तत्रार्पणं विषयसुखादिकं फलमनिच्छन् सर्वाः क्रियास्तस्मिन् परमगुरावर्पयति तत्प्रणिधानं समाधेस्तत्फललाभस्यच प्रकृष्ट उपायः॥

† ईश्वरस्य प्रणिधानात्समाधिलाभ इत्युक्तं। तत्रेश्वरस्य स्वरूपं प्रमाणं प्रभावं वाचकमुपासनाक्रमं तत्फलञ्च क्रमेण वक्तुमाह॥

meant those self-continuant conditions, or tendencies [—leading to their inevitable consequences—], which take the name of *áśaya* [—from the root *śí* 'to sleep,—] because they rest on the tablets of the mind until their fruit shall have ripened. [The Lord, to whom no such things are attributable, is declared to be] 'Untouched' by these—i. e. not affected by them during any of the three times, [—past, present, or future].*

b. A 'particular Spirit,'—i. e. one who is different from other spirits;—such is the force of the term here rendered 'particular.'†

The Lord upholds all things by His mere will.

c. 'The Lord' (*íśwara*)—i. e. [—from the root *śí* 'to possess power'—]who is accustomed to rule,—who is able to uphold the world by his mere will. Such is the nature of 'the Lord.'‡

d. Having thus stated the nature of the Lord, he now [§23. *b.*] states the proofs§ [that such a Being exists].

---

* क्लिश्नन्तीति क्लेशा अविद्यादयो वक्ष्यमाणाः। कर्म धर्माधर्मौ। विपाकाः कर्मफलानि जन्मायुर्भोगाः। आफलविपाकात् चित्तभूमौ शेरत इत्याशया वासनाख्याः संस्काराः। तैरपरामृष्टः त्रिष्वपि कालेषु न संस्पृष्टः।

† पुरुषविशेषः। अन्येभ्यः पुरुषेभ्यो विशिष्यत इति विशेषः।

‡ ईश्वरः। ईशनशीलः। इच्छामात्रेण सकलजगदुद्धरणक्षम इति स्वरूपमीश्वरस्येति॥

§ एवमीश्वरस्य स्वरूपमभिधाय प्रमाणमाह॥

तत्र निरतिशयं सर्वज्ञबीजम्॥ २५ ॥

Proof that there is such a Being as the Lord.

Aph. 25.—In Him does the germ of the omniscient become infinite.

a. 'In Him'—i. e. in that divine Being. The germ of omniscience is the less or more of the knowledge of the past, the future, &c. This is the germ, because like a germ it is the root [of what springs from it]. This [knowledge which in others is less or more] in Him, is infinite, or reaches its extreme limit. [And it is held to be a fair inference that Knowledge reaches the limit of Omniscience *somewhere*], for, properties that are capable of degrees, such as Parvitude and Magnitude, are [in particular instances] seen to have reached their extreme limits,—Parvitude, for example, in an Atom, and pre-eminent Magnitude in the Ether. So too Knowledge and the like, properties of the intellect, are seen admitting of degrees. They reach their extreme limit *somewhere*, and He in whom they are infinite is the Lord.*

b. Having thus declared the nature of the Lord, and the proof that such a Being exists, he next [§23. *b.*] declares His pre-eminence.†

---

* तत्र। तस्मिन् भगवति। सर्वज्ञत्वस्य यद्बीजं अतीतानागतादिग्रहणस्याल्पत्वं महत्त्वञ्च मूलत्वात् बीजमिव बीजं। तत्तत्र निरतिशयं काष्ठाप्राप्तं। दृष्टा ह्यल्पत्वमहत्त्वादीनां धर्माणां सातिशयानां काष्ठाप्राप्तिर्यथा परमाणावल्पत्वस्य आकाशे च परममहत्त्वस्य। एवं ज्ञानादयो ऽपि चित्तधर्मास्तारतम्येन परिदृश्यमानाः क्वचिन्निरतिशयतामासादयन्ति यत्रचैते निरतिशयास्स ईश्वर इति॥

† एवमीश्वरस्य स्वरूपं प्रमाणञ्चाभिधाय प्रभावमाह॥

स एष पूर्वेषामपि गुरुः कालेनानवच्छेदात्॥ २६ ॥

The pre-eminence of the Lord.

Aph. 26.—He is the preceptor even of the first, for He is not limited by time.

a. 'Of the first;'—that is to say, even of the earliest [of created beings], such as Brahmá, &c. He [the Lord] is the preceptor, or instructor; for *He* is not bounded by time, since He is without beginning,—and *these*, on the other hand, *are* limited by time because they *had* a beginning.*

b. Having thus declared the pre-eminence [of the Lord], he declares His name [§ 23. *b.*], with a view to its employment in devotion.†

तस्य वाचकः प्रणवः॥ २७ ॥

The mystical name of the Lord.

Aph. 27. His name is Glory.

a. 'His,'—i. e. of the Lord as thus defined [§24], the name, or appellation, is 'Glory' *(praṇava)*, [which is the technical term employed in speaking of the mystical name] '*Om.*'‡

b. And of the two [—i. e. of the Lord and this name—] the relation, as 'denoted and denoter,' is eternal. It is convention-

---

* पूर्वेषां। आद्यानां ब्रह्मादीनामपि स गुरुरुपदेष्टा यतस्स कालेनानवच्छिद्यते अनादित्वात्। तेषां पुनरादिमत्त्वादस्ति कालेनावच्छेदः॥

† एवं प्रभावमुक्त्वोपासनोपयोगाय वाचकमाह॥

‡ इत्थमुक्तस्वरूपस्य तस्येश्वरस्य वाचकोऽभिधायकः प्रणव ओङ्कारः।

ally *declared,*—but not *made* by any one. Just in like manner as the actual relation between a father and his son is *declared* [and not *created*] by some one who says "This is that one's father, and that is this one's son."*

c. He next speaks of worship† [—§23. *b.*]

तज्जपस्तदर्थभावनम्॥ २८ ॥

How the name of the Lord is to be used in worship.

Aph. 28.—Its repetition [should be made, and also] reflection on its signification.

a. 'Its',—i. e. of this mystical name, consisting of three and a half prosodial moments [viz: $(a=2)+(u=1)+(m=\frac{1}{2})=(om=3\frac{1}{2})$], the repetition, or proper pronunciation; and reflection on, or re-iterated mental attention to, its signification—viz: the Lord,—is a means of concentrating the thoughts; therefore it is here stated that the follower of the *Yoga* ought to repeat the mystical name and to reflect upon its import, with a view to the effecting of abstract Meditation.‡

b. He next mentions the fruits [§23. *b.*] of such worship.§

---

* तयोश्च वाच्यवाचकभावलक्षणस्सम्बन्धो नित्यः। सङ्केतेन प्रकाश्यते नतु केनचित्क्रियते। यथा पितृपुत्रयोर्विद्यमानः सम्बन्धो ऽस्यायं पितास्यायं पुत्र इति केनचित्प्रकाश्यते॥

† उपासनामाह॥

‡ तस्य सार्द्धत्रिमात्रस्य प्रणवस्य जपो यथावदुच्चारणं तद्वाच्यस्येश्वरस्य भावनं पुनःपुनश्चेतसि निवेशनं एकाग्रताया उपायो ऽतस्समाधिसिद्धये योगिना प्रणवो जप्यस्तदर्थश्च भावनीय इत्युक्तं भवति॥

§ उपासनायाः फलमाह॥

ततः प्रत्यक्चेतनाधिगमो ऽप्यन्तरायाभावश्च ॥ २९ ॥

Aph. 29.—Thence comes the knowledge of the rightly intelligent [Spirit], and the absence of obstacles.

a. 'The rightly intelligent [Spirit]'—i. e. the Spirit possessed of knowledge,—He being an intelligence who rightly knows,—i. e. who knows in an opposite, or inverse way, [as contradistinguished from mortals, whose understanding—as explained under § 5.—is supposed to flow out and become modified by objects. Such a process of gaining knowledge, being regarded as undesirable in the case of mortals, is not to be imagined to belong to the Lord, who is therefore said to know in some opposite way]. There accrues to him [the ascetic] a knowledge, a complete apprehension, of Him,* [through the practice recommended in §23].

b. The obstacles [to the attainment of the end in view] will be mentioned. The absence of these means the exclusion of their power.†

c. Now, which are those *obstacles?* This being a point in doubt, he proceeds to remark as follows.‡

---

* प्रतीपं विपरीतं अञ्चति विजानातीति प्रत्यक्। स चासौ चेतनश्चेति प्रत्यक्चेतनो विद्वान् पुरुषः। तस्य अधिगमो ज्ञानं स्वरूपतो ऽस्य भवति।

† अन्तराया वक्ष्यमाणास्तेषामभावः शक्तिप्रतिबन्धो भवति ॥

‡ अथ के ते ऽन्तराया इत्याशङ्कायामाह ॥

व्याधिस्त्यानसंशयप्रमादालस्याविरतिभ्रान्तिदर्शनालब्धभूमि-
कत्वानवस्थितत्वानि चित्तविक्षेपास्तेऽन्तरायाः ॥ ३० ॥

The obstacles of the ascetic.

Aph. 30.—Sickness, languor, doubt, carelessness, laziness, addiction to objects [of sense], erroneous perception, failure to attain any stage [of abstraction], and instability [in the state when attained],—these distractions of the mind are obstacles [in the way of the ascetic].

a. These nine, prevailing through the power of the passionate and dark qualities [—the two which are opposed to the element of pure or good in the phenomenal world—] become distractions of the mind :—that is to say, the mind is distracted by these which are opposed to the mind's concentrating itself on any point.*

Sickness.

b. Among these, 'Sickness,' is a fever, or the like, caused by disorder of the humours.†

Languor.

c. 'Languor' is the mind's inactivity.‡

Doubt.

d. 'Doubt' is a [sort of] notion that leans to both alternatives. As, for example, [where one hesitates] "Is the *Yoga* practicable [e. g. for me the doubter], or is it not?"§

---

* नवैते रजस्तमोवशात् प्रवर्त्तमानाश्चित्तस्य विक्षेपा भवन्ति। तैरेकाग्रताविरोधिभिश्चित्तं विक्षिप्यत इत्यर्थः॥

† तत्र व्याधिर्धातुवैषम्यनिमित्तो ज्वरादिः॥

‡ स्त्यानमकर्मण्यता चित्तस्य॥

§ उभयकोट्यालम्बनं विज्ञानं संशयः। योगस्साध्यस्स्याद्वा नवेति॥

Carelessness. e. 'Carelessness' is a habit of inattention, —a listlessness about the effecting of abstract meditation.*

Laziness. f. 'Laziness' is a heaviness of the body and mind, which causes a want of exertion in the department of abstract meditation.†

Addiction to objects. g. 'Addiction to objects' *(avirati)* is a greediness consisting in attachment of the mind to objects of sense.‡

Erroneous perception. h. 'Erroneous perception' is a mistaken notion [§8. *a.*] such as the notion that the thing is silver when it is mother o'pearl.§

Failure to attain any stage of abstraction. i. By 'failure to attain any stage' we mean the failing, for some reason or another, to attain to, or arrive at, the state of abstract meditation.‖

Instability. j. 'Instability' is, even when the state of abstract meditation has been reached, the mind's not continuing steadily therein.¶

---

* प्रमादोऽनुष्ठानशीलता समाधिसाधने औदासीन्यम्॥

† आलस्यं कायचित्तयोर्गुरुत्वं योगविषये प्रवृत्त्यभावहेतुः॥

‡ अविरतिश्चित्तस्य विषयसम्प्रयोगात्मा गर्द्धः॥

§ भ्रान्तिदर्शनं शुक्तिकायां रजतत्ववद्विपर्ययज्ञानम्॥

‖ अलब्धभूमिकत्वं कुतश्चिन्निमित्तात्समाधिभूमेरलाभ असम्प्राप्तिः॥

¶ अनवस्थितत्वं लब्धायामपि समाधिभूमौ चित्तस्य तु तत्राप्रतिष्ठा॥

k. These [§ 30.] are called 'obstacles' because, as they present themselves, they oppose concentration or meditation.*

l. In order to declare other obstacles also, which cause distraction of mind, he says† :—

दुःखदौर्मनस्याङ्गमेजयत्वश्वासविक्षेपसहभुवः॥ ३१॥

Aph. 31.—Grief, Distress, Trembling, and Sighing, are accompaniments of the distractions.

a. When, from whatever cause, distractions [such as enumerated in § 30.] have arisen, then these, viz. Grief, &c. [§ 31.] come on.‡

Grief. *b.* Among these [§ 31.] 'Grief' is a modification of mind, resulting from [other] mental affections and characterised by annoyance, in consequence of which annoyance sentient creatures exert themselves for its removal.§

Distress. *c.* 'Distress' is a tremulousness of mind, arising either from external or internal causes.‖

---

* एते समाधेरेकाग्रताया यथायोगं प्रतिपक्षत्वादन्तराया इत्युच्यन्ते॥

† चित्तविक्षेपकारकानन्यानप्यन्तरायान् प्रतिपादयितुमाह॥

‡ कुतश्चिन्निमित्तादुत्पन्नेषु विक्षेपेषु एते दुःखादयः प्रवर्त्तन्ते॥

§ तत्र दुःखं चित्तस्य राजसः परिणामो बाधनालक्षणो यद्बाधात् प्राणिनस्तदपघाताय प्रवर्त्तन्ते॥

‖ दौर्मनस्यं बाह्याभ्यन्तरैः कारणैर्मनसश्चाञ्चल्यम्॥

Trembling. *d.* ‘Trembling’ *(angamejayatwa)* is a shaking of the whole body which prevents steadiness either in prescribed postures or in mind.*

Sighing. *e.* ‘Sighing’ *(śwása)* is an excessive entrance of air into the body. An excessive expiration of air from the body, is what is meant by *praśwása.*†

f. These [§ 31.], prevailing along with the distractions [enumerated in § 30.], are to be excluded by means of ‘exercise’ [§ 13.] and ‘dispassion’ [§ 15.] as aforesaid; and therefore it is that they are mentioned here.‡

h. He now mentions another method for the prevention of the obstacles [§ 30.] together with their supervenients [§ 31.].§

तत्प्रतिषेधार्थमेकतत्त्वाभ्यासः ॥ ३२ ॥

Means of combating distractions. *Aph.* 32.—For the prevention thereof let one truth be dwelt upon.

a. For the prevention, or hindrance, of these distractions, one should dwell upon, or again and again confine the attention, to

---

* अङ्गमेजयत्वं सर्वाङ्गीणो वेपथुरासनमनःस्थैर्ययोर्बाधकः ॥

† श्वासो देहान्तर्वायोरधिकः प्रवेशः । प्रश्वासो देहाद्वायोरधिकनिर्गमः ॥

‡ त एते विक्षेपैस्सह प्रवर्त्तमाना यथोदिताभ्यासवैराग्याभ्यां निरोद्धव्या इत्येषामुपदेशं ॥

§ सोपद्रवविक्षेपप्रतिषेधार्थमुपायान्तरमाह ॥

one truth,—some accepted truth,—by force of which, when concentration on one point has taken place, the distractions subside.*

b. He next states another method, premising some mention of purifying processes which conduce to the perfecting of the mind.†

मैत्रीकरुणामुदितोपेक्षाणां सुखदुःखपुण्यापुण्यविषयाणां भावनातश्चित्तप्रसादनम्॥ ३३ ॥

Amiable habits recommended. *Aph.* 33.—Through the practising of benevolence, tenderness, complacency, and disregard towards objects [i. e. persons who are respectively in possession] of happiness, grief, virtue, and vice, the mind becomes purified.

a. 'Benevolence' is good-heartedness; 'tenderness' is compassion; 'complacency' is sympathetic joy; 'disregard' is indifference. He should exercise these, respectively, towards the happy, the grieved, the virtuous, and the vicious. That is to say, when people are happy, he should show benevolence, saying, "Blessings on their joy!",—and not [show] envy. When people are grieved, he should show tenderness, saying "By what means, verily, can they be freed from their grief?"—and not [show] a disposition to stand aloof. And when people are virtuous, he

* तेषां विक्षेपाणां प्रतिषेधार्थं निषेधार्थमेकस्मिन् कस्मिंश्चिदभिमते तत्त्वे अभ्यासश्चेतसः पुनःपुनर्निवेशनं कुर्य्यात् यद्बलात् प्रत्युदितायामेकाग्रतायां विक्षेपाः प्रशममुपयान्ति।

† इदानीं चित्तसंस्कारापादकपरिकर्मकथनपूर्वकमुपायान्तरमाह॥

should exhibit complacency, by sympathetically rejoicing in their virtue,—and not [show] aversion by saying "What!—are these forsooth *virtuous?*" And in regard to the vicious he should practise simply indifference, showing neither sympathy nor aversion.*

b. In the aphorism, by the words 'happiness' 'grief', &c., are denoted those to whom these belong. So, in this manner, by the purifying influences of friendliness, &c., the mind being rendered cheerful, the production of abstract meditation takes place readily.†

c. This purifying process is an external one [and not an intimate portion of the *Yoga* itself]. As, in arithmetic, in effecting the calculations of questions of Alligation, &c. the operations of Addition &c., are valuable [not so much in themselves, but] as aids in effecting the *important* matter, so by exercising benevo-

---

* मैत्री सौहार्दं । करुणा कृपा । मुदिता हर्षः । उपेक्षा औदासीन्यं । एता यथाक्रमं सुखितेषु दुःखितेषु पुण्यवत्सु अपुण्यवत्सु च विभावयेत् । तथाहि । सुखितेषु साध्वेषां सुखित्वमिति मैत्रीं कुर्य्यान्नत्वीर्ष्याम् । दुःखितेषु कथन्नु नामैषां दुःखविमुक्ति स्यादिति कृपामेव कुर्य्यान्न ताटस्थ्यं । पुण्यवत्सु च पुण्यानुमोदनेन हर्षं कुर्य्यान्नतु किमेते पुण्यवन्त इति द्वेषं । अपुण्यवत्सु चौदासीन्यमेव भावयेन्नानुमोदनं न द्वेषम् ॥

† सूत्रे सुखदुःखादिशब्दैस्तद्वन्तः प्रतिपादिताः । तदेवं मैत्र्यादिपरिकर्मणा चित्ते प्रसीदति सुखेन समाधेराविर्भावो भवति ॥

lence, &c., which are [moods of mind] opposed to aversion and covetousness, the mind, in which composure has [thereby] been produced, becomes fitted for meditation—that 'in which there is distinct recognition of an object' [§ 17.], &c. Covetousness and aversion are the very chief raisers of distractions:—if therefore these be radically extirpated, then, through its composure [and freedom from distraction], the mind [the more readily] becomes concentrated on one point.*

d. He mentions another expedient.†

प्रच्छर्दनविधारणाभ्यां वा प्राणस्य ॥ ३४ ॥

Another expedient for combating distraction.

Aph. 34.—[Or, he may combat distractions] by forcibly expelling and by restraining the breath.

Regulation of the breath.

a. The 'expelling' of the breath is the vomiting or emitting it [by a slow but complete expiration]. The 'restraining' it, is the stopping it [by shutting the mouth and closing both nostrils with the fingers of the right hand]. And this, we mean to say, takes place after *inhalation* [—though men-

---

* परिकर्मचैतद्बाह्यं कर्म। यथा गणिते मिश्रकादिव्यवहारगणितनिष्पत्तये सङ्कलितादिकर्मोपकारकत्वेन प्रधानकर्मनिष्पत्तये प्रभवति एवं द्वेषरागादिप्रतिपक्षभूतमैत्र्यादिभावनया समुत्पादितप्रसादं चित्तं सम्प्रज्ञातादिसमाधियोग्यं सम्पद्यते। रागद्वेषावेव मुख्यतया विक्षेपमुत्पादयतः। तौ चेत्समूलमुन्मूलितौ स्यातां तदा प्रसन्नत्वान्मनसो भवत्येकाग्रता॥

† उपायान्तरमाह॥

F

tioned in the aphorism as if immediately following *expiration*—], because, after expelling the breath, it is impossible to *restrain* it without [having made a previous] inhalation. Thus, then, the regulation of the breath [*prâṇâyâma*], being of three descriptions according to the distinction of 'expiration' (*rechaka*), 'inspiration' (*púraka*), and 'restraining' (*kumbhaka*), causes steadiness of the mind, and its concentration in a single direction.*

b. He states another means of steadiness.†

विषयवती वा प्रवृत्तिरुत्पन्ना स्थितिनिबन्धिनी ॥ ३५ ॥

Another expedient. *Aph.* 35.—Or a sensuous immediate cognition, being produced, may serve as a cause of the steadiness [of the mind].

a. To complete the sentence, we must supply 'of the mind.'‡

b. Objects of sense are odour, savour, colour, touch, and sound. Wherever these exist as fruits, that case of perception, or especially immediate cognition, is sensuous:—and this, when it is excited, causes fixation of the mind.§

---

* प्राणस्य प्रच्छर्दनं वमनं रेचनमिति यावत्। विधारणं कुम्भकं। तच्चार्थात् पूरकानन्तरं। रेचकोत्तरं पूरकं विना विधारणासम्भवात्। तदेवं रेचकपूरककुम्भकभेदेन त्रिविधः प्राणायामश्चित्तस्य स्थितिमेकाग्रतां निबध्नाति ॥

† स्थितिनिबन्धान्तरमाह ॥

‡ मनस इति वाक्यशेषः ॥

§ विषया गन्धरसरूपस्पर्शशब्दास्ते विद्यन्ते फलत्वेन यस्यां

Mystical sense-perception. *c.* To explain:—in the case of him who fixes his mind on the tip of his nose, there arises a perception of celestial odour. [If he fix his mind] on the tip of the tongue, in like manner, there is a perception of savour; on the fore-part of the palate, a perception of colour; on the middle of the tongue, a perception of the touch; on the root of the tongue, a perception of the sound. Thus, then, through this or that organ, the perception arising of this or that celestial sense-object becomes a cause of the mind's concentration in one direction.*

d. He mentions another expedient of the like description.†

विशोका वा ज्योतिष्मती ॥ ३६ ॥

Another expedient. *Aph.* 36.—Or a luminous [immediate cognition, being produced,] free from sorrow, [may serve as a cause of the steadiness of the mind].

a. To complete the aphorism, we must supply 'an immediate

सा विषयवती प्रवृत्तिः प्रकृष्टा साक्षात्काररूपा वृत्तिः। सा-चोत्पन्ना मनसस्स्थैर्यं करोति ॥

* तथाहि। नासाग्रे चित्तं धारयतो दिव्यगन्धसंविदुपजायते। तादृश्येव जिह्वाग्रे रससंवित्। तात्वग्रे रूपसंवित्। जिह्वामध्ये स्पर्शसंवित्। जिह्वामूले शब्दसंवित्। तदेवं तत्तदिन्द्रियद्वारेण तस्मिन् तस्मिन् दिव्ये विषये जायमाना संवित् चित्तस्यैकाग्रताया हेतुर्भवति ॥

† एवंविधमेवोपायान्तरमाह ॥

cognition, being produced, may serve as a cause of the steadiness of the mind.'*

b. Here, by the word 'lumen' *(jyotis)* is meant the light that consists of the Pure element [out of the three elementary qualities that constitute the phenomenal]. A luminous immediate cognition [§ 35. *b.*] is that in which this [Pure element] is excellent, abundant, exceeding.†

c. 'Free from sorrow,'—that is to say, that cause of the steadiness of the mind in respect of which [agency] all sorrow, which [—see *Sánkhya Lecture,* § 61.—] is a modification of the Passionate [or *foul* element of the phenomenal universe], is removed by virtue of the exercise of the 'beatific'‡ [degree of meditation—§ 17. *g.*,—where the ascetic, not yet liberated from the phenomenal, is nearly freed from the two coarser of its three chains].

Dwelling on the inner light of the heart.

d. The meaning is this, that, on the disappearance of all 'modifications' [§ 5.] through the beholding of perfect knowledge, steadiness takes place in the mind of him who, in the midst of the lotus-cup of his heart, broods on the Pure element of thought [spread out in the heart] like the milky ocean when its waves are stilled.§

---

* प्रवृत्तिरुत्पन्ना चित्तस्य स्थितिनिबन्धिनीति वाक्यशेषः ॥

† अत्र ज्योतिःशब्देन सात्त्विकः प्रकाश उच्यते। स प्रशस्तो भूयानतिशयवांश्च विद्यते यस्यां सा ज्योतिष्मती प्रवृत्तिः ॥

‡ विशोका विगतसुखमयसत्त्वाभ्यासबलात् शोको रजःपरिणामरूपो यस्याः सा चेतसः स्थितिनिबन्धिनी ॥

§ अयमर्थः। हृत्पद्मपुटमध्ये प्रशान्तकल्लोलक्षीरोदधि-

e. By means of exhibiting another expedient, he declares an object [worthy of being meditated] in the meditation 'in which there is distinct recognition of an object'*—[§ 17].

वीतरागविषयं वा चित्तम्॥ ३७॥

Dwelling on admirable examples.

Aph. 37.—Or the thought, taking as its object some one devoid of passion, [may find what will serve as a cause of the steadiness of the mind].

a. To complete the aphorism we must supply 'may [find what will] serve as a cause of the steadiness of the mind.'†

b. 'Devoid of passion,' i. e., who has abandoned all desire for objects of sense,—like Sanaka and others. [The mind, we repeat, may be steadied by the expedients previously mentioned,] or the thoughts of the Yogí, directed to *this* [—i. e. to one devoid of passion as Sanaka was—], becomes fixed;—that is to say, the unimpassioned thought becomes more firmly steady through reflecting on one whose thoughts are devoid of passion.‡

प्रख्यं चित्तसत्त्वं भावयतः प्रज्ञालोकात् सर्ववृत्तिक्षये चेतसः स्थैर्यमुत्पद्यत इति॥

* उपायान्तरप्रदर्शनद्वारेण सम्प्रज्ञातसमाधेर्विषयं दर्शयति॥

† मनसः स्थितिनिबन्धनम्भवतीति वाक्यशेषः॥

‡ वीतरागः परित्यक्तविषयाभिलाषस्सनकादिः। तद्विषयकं वा योगिचित्तं निबद्धं भवति विरक्तचित्तस्य भावनया विरक्तं चित्तं दृढस्थितये भवतीत्यर्थः॥

c. He mentions another expedient of this description.*

स्वप्ननिद्राज्ञानालम्बनं वा ॥ ३८ ॥

Recourse had to dreaming and sleeping. *Aph.* 38.—Or the dwelling on knowledge [that presents itself] in dream, or in sleep, [may serve as a cause of the steadiness of the mind].

Dreaming defined. *a.* 'Dream' is that wherein the soul is affected through the mind alone, when the modifications of the external organs of sense have departed.†

b. 'Sleep' has already been defined‡ [—see § 10.].

c. [We say, then, that] knowledge dependent on dream, or dependent on sleep, when dwelt upon, causes steadiness of mind,§—[there being in either case nothing to distract the attention].

d. Since [different] men have different tastes, on whatever thing the Yogí places his faith, by meditating on that same thing he may attain what he wants [—viz. steadiness of mind] :—in order to declare this, he states as follows.||

---

* एवंविधमुपायान्तरमाह ।

† प्रत्यस्तमितबाह्येन्द्रियवृत्तेः मनोमात्रेणैव यत्र भोक्तृत्वमात्मनः स स्वप्नः ॥

‡ निद्रा उक्तलक्षणा ॥

§ स्वप्नालम्बनं निद्रालम्बनं वा ज्ञानमालम्ब्यमानं चेतसः स्थितिं करोति ॥

|| नानारुचित्वात्प्राणिनां यस्मिन् कस्मिंश्चिद्वस्तुनि यो

यथाभिमतध्यानाद्वा ॥ ३९ ॥

Anything you please may be dwelt upon to steady the mind.

Aph. 39.—Or [the steadying of the mind may be effected] by pondering anything that one approves.

a. [That is to say] the mind becomes steadied when any object that one prefers is pondered,—whether external, as the Moon or the like, or internal, as a congeries of arteries or the like.*

The fruit of meditation.

b. Having thus exhibited the means [of accomplishing meditation], in order to exhibit the fruits, he proceeds to remark.†

परमाणुपरममहत्त्वान्तोऽस्य वशीकारः ॥ ४० ॥

To apprehend the infinitely small or great.

Aph. 40.—His mastery extends to the atomic and to the infinite.

a. The ascetic, effecting, by these methods, steadiness of mind, obtains, through meditation on subtile objects, unresisted mastery as far as the Atoms;—that is to say, his mind, in [dealing with] subtile objects, even as far as the Atoms [which elude the cognizance of ordinary perspicacity], is nowhere baffled. In like

---

गिनः श्रद्धा भवति तस्य ध्यानेनापि भवतीष्टसिद्धिरिति प्रतिपादयितुमाह ॥

* यथाभिमते वस्तुनि बाह्ये चन्द्रादावाभ्यन्तरे नाडीचक्रादौ वा भाव्यमाने चेतः स्थिरीभवति ॥

† एवमुपायान् प्रदर्श्य फलप्रदर्शनार्थमाह ॥

manner no mental obstacle arises anywhere to him meditating the gross, even to the extent of infinite magnitude,—as the Ether, for example;—but everywhere he is uncontrolled,—such is the meaning.*

b. Of the mind thus by these methods rectified, what is the aspect [or actual condition]? To this he replies.†

क्षीणवृत्तेरभिजातस्येव मणेर्ग्रहीतृग्रहणग्राह्येषु तत्स्थतदञ्जनतापत्तिः ॥ ४१ ॥

The state of the mind properly intent on a single object.

Aph. 41.—To that [mind] whose 'modifications' [—all save that there remains some one object of meditation—] have disappeared, there occurs, as [occurs] to a noble gem [—e. g. rock-crystal, when brought into conjunction with a coloured substance—], when intent on any one out of these—viz.—the perceiver, the perception, and the perceivable,—a tingeing thereby.

a. That is to say—to that [mind] whose 'modifications' [§ 5.]

---

* एभिरुपायैश्चित्तस्थैर्यम्भावयतो योगिनः सूक्ष्मविषयभावनाद्वारेण परमाण्वन्तो वशीकारोऽप्रतिघातरूपो जायते क्वचित् परमाणुपर्यन्ते सूक्ष्मे विषये अस्य मनो न प्रतिहन्यत इत्यर्थः। एवं स्थूलमाकाशादिपरममहत्त्वपर्यन्तम्भावयतो न क्वचिच्चेतःप्रतिघात उत्पद्यते किन्तु सर्वत्र स्वातन्त्र्यम्भवतीत्यर्थः ॥

† एवमेभिरुपायस्संस्कृतस्य चेतसः कीदृशं रूपम्भवतीत्याह ॥

have disappeared, which has repelled all modifications *except* that which has to be pondered,—which has accomplished that concentration 'in which there is distinct recognition'* [of a single object to the exclusion of all others,—§ 17.].

b. 'Out of [the three viz.] the perceiver, the perception, and the perceivable'—i. e. Soul, the organs of sense, and the [five] elements.†

c. 'To it [—the thought—] intent on any one [of these §41, *b.*—] there occurs a tingeing thereby.' By 'being intent thereon' we mean attending to that alone. 'A tingeing thereby,'—i. e. the [thought's] coming to consist thereof [by taking the colour or character of the object as its own];—the coming to be of the same description;—that is to say, it [—the thought—] becomes modified into the aspect of that‡ [which is thought upon].

d. He mentions an illustration. To the noble—i. e. pure [transparent and colourless]—gem, such a gem as rock-crystal or the like, there occurs this or that colour in consequence of its being the receptacle of this or that colour, [—as when the red or other colour of flowers has place within a crystal vase—]. In like manner, to the stainless pure element of thought [§36. *d.*]

---

* क्षीणा वृत्तयो यस्य तस्य निरुद्धध्येयातिरिक्तवृत्तेः सम्पन्नसम्प्रज्ञातयोगस्येत्यर्थः ॥

† ग्रहीतृग्रहणग्राह्येषु पुरुषेन्द्रियभूतेषु ॥

‡ तत्स्थतदञ्जनतापत्तिः। तत्स्थत्वं तदेकाग्रता। तदञ्जनता तन्मयत्वं। तथाविधा समापत्तिः तद्रूपपरिणामो भवतीत्यर्थः ॥

there occurs the hue of this or that, through the adjacent hue of this or that thing which is meditated upon.*

e. 'The perceived, the perception, and the perceiver'—such is the inverse order in which these are to be understood [—instead of the order adopted in the aphorism—], because it is on 'the perceived' [—the external or objective—] that meditation is first fixed,† [—see §17. *e.* &c].

f. He now states [in three aphorisms] a fourfold division of the abovementioned [§41] change‡ [of the mind into the likeness of what it ponders].

शब्दार्थज्ञानविकल्पैस्सङ्कीर्णा सवितर्का ॥ ४२ ॥

The first stage of the mind properly intent.

Aph. 42.—This [change of the mind into the likeness of what is pondered—§41—], when mixed up of the fancy of the 'word,' the 'meaning,' and the 'knowledge,' is [technically termed] the 'argumentative.'

a. A 'Word,' is what is apprehended by the organ of hearing, or [in the technical language of the grammarians] a manifestation§ *(sphoṭa).*

---

* दृष्टान्तमाह । अभिजातस्य निर्मलस्य मणेः स्फटिकादिमणेः तत्तद्रूपाश्रयवशात् तत्तद्रूपापत्तिः । एवं निर्मलस्य चित्तसत्त्वस्य तत्तद्भावनीयवस्तूपरागात् तत्तद्रूपापत्तिः ।

† ग्राह्यग्रहणग्रहीतृष्विति व्यत्यासेन योजनीयं यतः प्रथमं ग्राह्यनिष्ठ एव समाधिरिति ॥

‡ इदानीमुक्ताया एव समापत्तेश्चतुर्विधभेदमाह ॥

§ श्रोत्रेन्द्रियग्राह्यः स्फोटो वा शब्दः ।

b. The 'Meaning' i. e. the thing meant by a sound or word] is a genus [—such as 'cow,' 'horse,'—] &c.,* [see *Sáhitya Darpaṇa* §12].

c. 'Knowledge,' is a modification of the understanding [—see §5 and 6—] where the quality of Purity prevails† [—to the suppression of the elements of Passion and Darkness,—see §17. *g*].

d. A 'Fancy' has been already defined‡ [in *Aph.* 9].

e. 'Mixed up of these'—i. e. in which the three—viz. the 'Word,' &c., [§42],—by mutually commingling, appear in an [ambiguous and] fanciful shape,—in the shape [at once] of the *word* 'cow,' [for example], the *thing* 'cow,' and the *notion* 'cow,'—this is what is called [technically] 'the argumentative' (*savitarka*) change§ [of the mind reflecting a mixed object of thought—while the attention is divided among the sound, the thing signified, and the knowledge of the thing].

f. He now mentions that 'non-argumentative' [affection of the mind] which is the opposite of the one just defined|| [§42].

---

* अर्थो जात्यादिः ।

† ज्ञानं सत्त्वप्रधाना बुद्धिवृत्तिः ।

‡ विकल्प उक्तलक्षणः ।

§ तैस्सङ्कीर्णा । यस्यामेते शब्दादयः परस्पराध्यासेन विकल्परूपेण त्रयः प्रतिभासन्ते गौरिति शब्दो गौरित्यर्थो गौरिति ज्ञानमित्यनेनाकारेण सा सवितर्का समापत्तिरित्युच्यते ।

|| उक्तलक्षणविपरीतां निर्वितर्कामाह ।

स्मृतिपरिशुद्धौ स्वरूपशून्येवार्थमात्रनिर्भासा निर्वितर्का ॥ ४३ ॥

The second stage of the mind properly intent.

Aph. 43.—On the clearing off of the memory [of the word and the sense attached to it by convention], the [mental] display only of the thing itself as if of something indefinite [and no longer referred to any term—no longer regarded as being what is meant by the word 'cow,' or what is meant by the word 'horse,' &c.—], this [affection of the mind which no longer reflects a mixed object of thought—§42—] is that which is called [technically] the 'non-argumentative.'

a. 'Of the memory'—i. e. of the memory of the convention as to the sense of the word. 'The clearing off'—i. e. the departure. When this takes place, the change [of the mind] when it reveals the thing itself alone, as if devoid of any character [which would suggest a term as applicable to it],—when it [the mind in its changed state—§41—] is employed about the object to be pondered alone [without regard to its having any name], and thus clear of 'fancy' [—nothing being pondered but the actual thing itself—], is what is called the 'non-argumentative' [affection of the mind]; such is the meaning.*

b. In order to declare another division, he says:†—

---

* स्मृतेः। शब्दार्थसङ्केतस्मृतेः। परिशुद्धिरपगमस्तस्यां सत्यां स्वरूपशून्येव अर्थमात्रनिर्भासा ध्येयार्थमात्रावगाहिनी विकल्पशून्या समापत्तिर्निर्वितर्कसंज्ञेत्यर्थः।

† भेदान्तरं प्रतिपादयितुमाह॥

एतयैव सविचारानिर्विचाराच सूक्ष्मविषया व्याख्याता ॥ ४४ ॥

The third and fourth stages of the mind properly intent.

Aph. 44.—Just by this [mental affection under the two aspects explained in Aphorisms 42 and 43], that which is [technically termed] 'deliberative' *(sa-vichára)*, and [that termed] 'non-deliberative' *(nir-vichára)*, where the object [pondered,—instead of being gross as in these two preceding cases—] is 'subtile,' has been [sufficiently] explained; [—the distinction between this pair, out of the four referred to at §41 *f.*, being the same as that between the other pair].

a. Just by this mental affection, in the shape of the 'argumentative' [§42] and the 'non-argumentative' [§43], where the object is a 'gross' one [as contradistinguished from the 'subtile' objects,—see §44 *b.*—], the pair of mental affections also, in the shape of the 'deliberative' and the 'non-deliberative,' where the object is 'subtile,' has been explained.*

b. What sort [of mental affection] is that where the object is *subtile?* That [mental affection] is so called, the object whereof, such as the 'subtile elements' or the 'organs' [§17. *f.*], is subtile. By this [mention that the object, in the case of the latter pair,—§44, *a.*,—as 'subtile'] it is declared that in the former [pair] the object is 'gross,'—for [in truth] it is on the gross elements that it [—the former pair §42—43—] is dependent. That is [called] the 'deliberative' [§44] in which the 'subtile object' appears whether as the object of a question as to the name, the meaning, and the notion [§42], or apart from any such question, but yet as qualified by the characters of space and time, &c. That [on the

---

* एतयैव सवितर्कनिर्वितर्करूपया स्थूलविषयकसमापत्त्या सूक्ष्मविषयापि सविचारनिर्विचाररूपसमापत्तिद्वयी व्याख्याता।

other hand] is [called] the 'non-deliberative' [§44], in which the 'subtile object,' in the shape of the Subtile Elements or the Organs, independently of the properties of space and time, &c., is presented simply as the thing itself. It is of this [pair of mental modifications] alone that the objects are 'subtile'* [—and not of the other pair,—see §44. *a*].

c. In reply to the question how far [the term] 'where the object is subtile' [§44] [extends], he says:—†

सूक्ष्मविषयत्वञ्चालिङ्गपर्यवसानम् ॥ ४५ ॥

The limit of analysis. *Aph.* 45.—And 'the having a subtile object' ends with the Indissoluble.

a. This fact that has been mentioned of the 'deliberative' and the 'non-deliberative' mental affections [§44], that their object is a 'subtile' one [§44. *b*.], ends with the Indissoluble,—meaning, by the 'Indissoluble,' Nature, [that primordial principle—see Sánkhya Lecture §7—] which is nowhere resolved [into any thing underlying it],—or which [to take another etymological

---

* कीदृशी सूक्ष्मविषया। सूक्ष्मस्तन्मात्रेन्द्रियादिर्विषयो यस्यास्सा तथोक्ता। एतेन पूर्वस्यां स्थूलविषयत्वं प्रतिपादितम्भवति सा हि महाभूतालम्बना। शब्दार्थज्ञानविकल्पविषयत्वेन तद्रहितत्वेनच देशकालधर्माद्यवच्छिन्नः सूक्ष्मोऽर्थः प्रतिभाति यस्यां सा सविचारा। देशकालधर्मादिरहितो धर्मिमात्रतया सूक्ष्मोऽर्थस्तन्मात्रेन्द्रियरूपः प्रतिभाति यस्यां सा निर्विचारेत्यर्थः। अस्या एव सूक्ष्मविषयाः।

† किम्पर्यन्तसूक्ष्मविषय इत्याह।

explanation] declares or suggests nothing. It is at this point that 'the having a subtile object' ceases* [—seeing that, beyond this, there exists nothing more subtile lying further back].

b. To explain :—in the modification of the Qualities there arise four divisions—(1) that which has a diversified character, (2) that which has an undiversified character, (3) that which merely has a character, and (4) that which has not a character. [By] 'that which has a diversified character' *(viśishṭa-linga)* [is meant] the [gross] elements [Sánkhya Lecture §33]. [By] 'that which has an undiversified character' *(aviśishṭa-linga)* is meant the subtile elements and the organs [S. L. §25]. [By] 'that which merely has a character' *(linga-mátra)* is meant Intellect [S. L. §8]. [By] 'that which has not a characteristic attribute' *(alinga)* is meant the First Principle [S. L. §7] beyond which there is nothing subtile† [underlying or originating it.]

c. He next mentions, as the topic presents itself, the motive for [valuing] these mental affections [or tinges, §41.]‡

ता एव सबीजस्समाधिः॥ ४६ ॥

---

* सविचारनिर्विचारयोस्समापत्त्योर्यत्सूक्ष्मविषयत्वमुक्तं तदलिङ्गपर्यवसानं। न क्वचिल्लीयते न वा किञ्चिल्लिङ्गति गमयतीत्यलिङ्गं प्रधानं। तत्पर्यन्तं सूक्ष्मविषयत्वमिति।

† तथाहि। गुणानां परिणामे चत्वारि पर्वाणि विशिष्टलिङ्गमविशिष्टलिङ्गं लिङ्गमात्रमलिङ्गञ्चेति। विशिष्टलिङ्गं भूतानि। अविशिष्टलिङ्गं तन्मात्रेन्द्रियाणि। लिङ्गमात्रं बुद्धिः। अलिङ्गं प्रधानमिति नातः परं सूक्ष्ममस्तीत्युक्तं भवति।

‡ एतासां समापत्तीनां प्रकृते प्रयोजनमाह॥

What the aforesaid mental affections constitute.

Aph. 46.—These themselves constitute 'Meditation with its *seed*' [§17. *b*].

a. 'These themselves,' i. e. the mental affections above described. Meditation 'in which there is distinct recognition' [§17. *b.*] is called [meditation] 'with its seed'—i. e. that which is with a seed or with something to rest upon—because all these [varieties of mental affection which we have been treating of] have something to rest upon* [—which—see §17. *i.*—must eventually be deserted].

b. Now he states the fruit of the 'non-deliberative' [mental affection], seeing that, of the other mental affections, this 'non-deliberative' one [§44] is the fruit.†

निर्विचारवैशारद्येऽध्यात्मप्रसादः ॥ ४७ ॥

The fruit of this.

Aph. 47.—When wisdom has come, through the 'non-deliberative' [mental affection], there is spiritual clearness.

a. What we mean by 'non-deliberative' has been already explained‡ [—§44].

b. 'Wisdom' here stands for 'purity'.§

---

* ता एवोक्तलक्षणास्समापत्तयः । सह बीजेन आलम्बनेन वर्त्तत इति सबीजः सम्प्रज्ञातः समाधिरुच्यते सर्वासां सालम्बनत्वात् ॥

† अथेतरासां समापत्तीनां निर्विचारफलकत्वान्निर्विचारायाः फलमाह ॥

‡ व्याख्यातं निर्विचारत्वम् ॥

§ वैशारद्यं नैर्मल्यम् ॥

c. In comparison with the 'argumentative' [mental affection], when the object is a gross one, the 'non-argumentative' is the superior. In respect of that too the 'deliberative,' whose object is a subtile one, [is the superior]. In respect of this again the 'non-deliberative' [where the object is subtile, is the superior]. And when, in virtue of pre-eminent practice of this, there has arisen wisdom, or purity, then there is spiritual clearness. By 'spiritual' we mean what resides in the soul, or in the understanding. Such clearness [viz. spiritual clearness] arises [from the 'non-deliberative' mental affection with a subtile object]. And it is just this spiritual clearness which we mean by the firm steadfastness* [attained on the removal of distractions—§32].

d. [Well],—this having been attained, what next? To this he replies.†

ऋतम्भरा तत्र प्रज्ञा ॥ ४८ ॥

From spiritual clearness comes right knowledge.

Aph. 48.—In that case there is knowledge which holds to the truth.

a. By 'knowledge which holds to the true' we mean that

---

* सवितर्कां स्थूलविषयामपेक्ष्य निर्वितर्कायाः प्राधान्यं। ततोऽपि सूक्ष्मविषयायाः सविचारायाः। ततोऽपि निर्विचारायाः। तस्यास्तु प्रकृष्टाभ्यासवशाद्वैशारद्ये नैर्मल्ये सति अध्यात्मप्रसादः। आत्मनि बुद्धौ वर्त्तत इत्यध्यात्मं। तादृशः प्रसादस्समुपजायते। एतदेव चित्तस्य वैशारद्यं यत् स्थितौ दार्ढ्यमिति ॥

† तस्मिन् सति किम्भवतीत्याह ॥

H

knowledge which is never overshadowed by error,—which holds to the truth—i. e. to the real.*

b. 'In that case'—i. e. when *spiritual clearness* has been attained, this [true knowledge] takes place.†

c. And, through this rightly intelligent view, regarding everything as it really is, the *Yogí* attains to pre-eminent Concentration‡ [§2].

d. He now states the distinction of this from other [forms of] correct knowledge.§

श्रौतानुमानप्रज्ञाभ्यां सामान्यविषयाविशेषार्थत्वात् ॥ ४९ ॥

This knowledge differs from ordinary knowledge.

Aph. 49.—[This kind of knowledge differs] from the knowledge due to testimony and inference because the object of these two is not particulars but generals.

a. By 'testimony' we mean scriptural information. By 'inference' we mean what has been already defined [at §7 *a*]. The knowledge which arises from these two [sources of knowledge] has generals [and not individuals] as its object; for, neither testimony nor a [logical] sign [τεκμηρίον] is able, like a sense-organ, to convey a knowledge of particularities|| [meaning thereby the ultimate and no further explicable distinctions that exist between individuals generically similar and numerically different].

---

* ऋतं सत्यं बिभर्त्ति कदाचिदपि न विपर्ययेणाच्छाद्यते सा ऋतम्भरा प्रज्ञा ॥

† तत्र । अध्यात्मप्रसादे सति भवतीत्यर्थः ।

‡ तस्माच्च प्रज्ञालोकात्सर्वं यथावत्पश्यन् योगी प्रकृष्टं योगं प्राप्नोति ॥

§ अस्याः प्रज्ञान्तराद्वैलक्षण्यमाह ॥

|| श्रौतमागमज्ञानम् । अनुमानमुक्तलक्षणं । ताभ्यां या

b. On the other hand this meditative knowledge—that associated with the clearness which comes through the 'non-deliberative' [mental affection—§47]—differs from these two kinds of knowledge [§49 *a*], in its having individualities as its objects;—that is to say, [it differs from them] because its object is the individual 'subtile element' or the individual Soul itself.* [And so this knowledge, since its object is the particular, has an object other than that which belongs to testimony or inference].

c. Moreover, when this has been attained, one can discern with one's ordinary organs [even] minute things, hidden or very far off.†

d. The states the [especial] fruit of this correct knowledge.‡

तज्जस्संस्कारोऽन्यसंस्कारप्रतिबन्धी ॥ ५० ॥

One train of thought with one object, is to put an end to all other trains.

Aph. 50.—The train [of self-reproductive thought] resulting from this puts a stop to other trains.

a. The [self-reproductive] continuous flow [of thought—§18] produced by this [meditative] knowledge [§49] prevents other

---

जायते प्रज्ञा सा सामान्यविषया। नहि शब्दलिङ्गयोरिन्द्रियवद्विशेषप्रतिपत्तौ सामर्थ्यं ॥

* इयं पुनर्निर्विचारवैशारद्यसमुपेता समाधिप्रज्ञा ताभ्यां प्रज्ञाभ्यां विलक्षणा विशेषविषयत्वात्। विशेषः भूतसूक्ष्मगतः पुरुषगतो वा विषयो यस्य तस्मादित्यर्थः ॥

† किञ्चास्यां सूक्ष्मव्यवहितविप्रकृष्टस्य वस्तुनो लोकप्रत्यक्षेण ग्रहणमस्तीति ॥

‡ अस्याः प्रज्ञायाः फलमाह ॥

trains, whether they arise during relaxation or concentration;—is to say, it makes them incapable of producing their effects. It is for this reason that it is directed that one should addict himself to this kind of knowledge alone.*

b. Having thus described Meditation where there is distinct recognition [of an object §17], in order to declare that in which the distinct recognition is dropped [§17. *j.*], he says:—†

तस्यापि निरोधे सर्वनिरोधान्निर्बीजस्समाधिः ॥ ५१ ॥

Finally this last train of thought is to drop its object.

Aph. 51.—On the removal of this also, since there is removal of all [the mental modifications], the Meditation is 'without a seed.'

a. On the removal, i. e. on the dissolution, of this also,—i. e. of the meditation where there is distinct recognition of an object [§17],—when all the modifications of the mind [§5] have been resolved into their causes [or sources—as a jar, when broken, is resolved into the earth which it was made of—], so that there arises merely a continuous train [of thought self-reproductive], thereupon, as there is nothing but the negation 'This is not'—'This is not,'—meditation appears with relinquishment of the seed [§17. *b*];—on which taking place, the Soul is said to abide in its own nature pure—alone—emancipated.‡

---

* तया प्रज्ञया जनितो यस्संस्कारस्सोऽन्यान्व्युत्थानजान् समाधिजांश्च संस्कारान्प्रतिबध्नाति स्वकार्यकरणाक्षमान्करोतीत्यर्थः। अतस्तामेव प्रज्ञामभ्यसेदित्युक्तं भवति ॥

† एवं सम्प्रज्ञातसमाधिमभिधायासम्प्रज्ञातं वक्तुमाह ॥

‡ तस्यापि सम्प्रज्ञातस्यापि निरोधे प्रविलये सति सर्वासां चित्तवृत्तीनां स्वकारणे प्रविलयाद्या या संस्कारमात्रा वृत्ति-

Recapitulation.

b. Well then [—to recapitulate briefly—], having set forth the definition [§2] of 'Concentration' which is the subject of the work [§1], the explanation of the terms 'Modification of the mind' [§5] and the 'Prevention' thereof [§12], the definition of 'Exercise' [§13] and 'Dispassion' [§15], and having thus stated the nature of and the difference between these two expedients; then having stated the division of Concentration, into principal and secondary, by distinguishing it as 'Meditation in which there is distinct recognition' [§17] and that 'in which distinct recognition is lost [§18]; then having exhibited diffusively [§20—22] the expedients [for attaining to concentration], after premising an exposure of the 'Spurious semblance of concentration,' [§19]; then, with a view to exhibiting an *easy* method, having determined the nature of the Lord [§23—24], the proof of His existence [§25], His pre-eminence [§ 26], His name [§27], the order of His worship [§28] and the fruits thereof [§29]; then having described the distractions of the mind [§30] and their supervenients, grief &c. [§31], and diffusively, the means of combating these—viz. the dwelling upon some one truth [§ 32], the practice of benevolence &c. [§ 33], the regulation of the breath [§34], and other such means—viz. 'sensuous immediate cognitions &c.' [§35—39]—as are conducive to Meditation with or without distinct recognition of an object; having declared the mental affections [§ 41], with an eye to the winding up, with their definitions [§42—44], their fruits [§ 46—48], and their object [§49]; then by finally summing up, in regard to the Meditation with distinct recognition and that without distinct recognition of an object,—in words to the effect that Meditation without a seed is preceded by that which has a

---

रुद्देति तस्यां नेति नेति केवलं पर्युदसनान्निर्बीजसमाधिरा-विर्भवति यस्मिन् सति पुरुषः स्वरूपनिष्ठश्शुद्धः केवलो मुक्त इत्युच्यत इति ॥

seed §51, the chapter on Concentration has been expounded* [by Pantanjali.]

c. Thus is completed the First Book—that on Meditation—of the commentary, composed by the illustrious great king and governor King Bhojarájá, on the Aphorisms of Patanjali's System of the Yoga.†

Remarks. d. The commentator, it will be observed [—see Introduction, *b.*—], justifies Patanjali's undertaking to expound the *Yoga*, by citing a passage from the Veda [—the Náchiketa

---

* तदत्राधिकृतस्य योगस्य लक्षणं चित्तवृत्तिनिरोधपदानां व्याख्यानं अभ्यासवैराग्यलक्षणं तस्योपायद्वयस्य स्वरूपं भेदञ्चाभिधाय सम्प्रज्ञातासम्प्रज्ञातभेदेन योगस्य मुख्यामुख्यभेदमुक्त्वा योगाभासप्रदर्शनपूर्वकान् विस्तरेणोपायान् प्रदर्श्य सुगमोपायप्रदर्शनपरतयेश्वरस्य स्वरूपप्रमाणप्रभाववाचकोपासनाक्रमतत्फलानि निर्णीय चित्तस्य विक्षेपान् तत्सहभुवश्च दुःखादीन् विस्तरेण च तत्प्रतिषेधोपायानेकतत्त्वाभ्यासमैत्र्यादीन् प्राणायामादीन् सम्प्रज्ञातासम्प्रज्ञातपूर्वाङ्गभूतविषयवतीप्रवृत्तिरित्यादीनाख्यायोपसंहारद्वारेण समापत्तीस्वलक्षणाः सफलाः स्वस्वविषयसहिताश्चोक्त्वा सम्प्रज्ञातासम्प्रज्ञातयोरुपसंहारमभिधाय सबीजपूर्वको निर्बीजस्समाधिरिति व्याख्यातो योगपादः ॥

† इति श्रीमहाराजाधिराजश्रीभोजराजदेवविरचितायां पातञ्जलयोगशास्त्रसूत्रवृत्तौ प्रथमः समाधिपादः समाप्तः ॥

Upanishad—] recommendatory of the *Yoga*. The *Yoga*, therefore, under that name, was recognised antecedently to Patanjali, and is not to be regarded as an invention of his.

e. The term *Yoga*, we are told [§2], implies the hindering of the modifications of the thinking principle. All the six Hindú systems, five of which we have already partially examined, agree in regarding the distinction between Subject and Object as the most momentous of facts, and the emancipation of the former from all entanglement with the latter as the one desirable end. In their treatment of the Objective the systems differ, at least in appearance, more widely than in their treatment of the Subjective. The Vedánta denies reality—or most grudgingly allows any thing of reality—to the Objective. The Nyáya accords to it a reality co-ordinate with that of the Subject, giving impartially the name of Substance to both. The Sánkhya steers a middle course between these two. It treats the Objective as an aggregate of *qualities*, which exist as *such* but not as substances. In this respect, the Sánkhya comes even nearer than the Vedánta to Bishop Berkeley. The Yoga, as far as we have seen, concurs with the Sánkhya on this point. While the systems thus differ in regard to the objective or Material, they all agree, on the other hand, in regarding the Subject *(átman)*—call it Soul, or Spirit,—as a self-dependant reality. The only dispute here is, whether Soul, or Spirit, is one or manifold. The Vedánta holds that it is one; the other systems, so far as we have yet seen, that it is manifold. It is to be observed that nowhere in any of the systems does the notion of a *created* spirit present itself. The Vedánta, availing itself of a sufficiently loose analogy, speaks of one Soul pervading all bodies as one thread might pervade a necklace of golden, silver, and earthen, beads; while the Sánkhya urges the objection that if Soul were but one, then all would be happy when one is happy, all would die, when one died, and so on, which is contrary to experience, [Sánkhya Lecture §48 and 45]. But, whether Soul be one or manifold, every one of the systems holds it to be self-dependant. Soul is the *substance*—beneath which there stands nothing;—and the pity, in the estimation of Hindú philosophy, is, that anything should stand *above* it,—any more than beneath it. It ought to stand alone—apart from everything phenomenal.

f. In order to repel the transient or phenomenal, according to the *Yoga* [§ 12] we must have recourse to exercise and dispassion, or asceticism and mortification.

g. By means of ascetic exercises and the mortification of all desires, the mind is supposed to attain to a state of undisturbed Meditation [§ 17], where some one single object is pondered, to the exclusion of all others. But as the practised swimmer parts with his last cork or bladder, so the soul of the ascetic must in due course part with every object, and at length meditate without any object at all [§ 18]. To effect this being a matter of difficulty, devotion to *the Lord* [§ 23] is recommended as a comparatively easy method. In admitting the existence of a Divine Being *(íśwara)* in whom the good qualities belonging to man reach their limit, the Yoga, hence named the *seśwara sánkhya*, differs from the Sánkhya of Kapila, which is known as the *niríśwara*.

h. As the ascetic is exposed to obstacles, these are discussed by Patanjalí [§ 30—31], and means for combating them are indicated [§32—39].

i. When all obstacles have been thus removed, the mind is supposed to be as free from all contamination of the phenomenal as the pure crystal is free from the red colour which *seems* to belong to it while a rose is seen athwart it.

END OF BOOK I.

THE APHORISMS

OF THE

YOGA PHILOSOPHY,

OF

PATANJALI

WITH

ILLUSTRATIVE EXTRACTS FROM THE COMMENTARY

BY

BHOJA RÁJA.

BOOK II.

PRINTED FOR THE USE OF THE BENARES COLLEGE
BY ORDER OF GOVT. N. W. P.

[1st EDITION, 400 COPIES, *Price* 8 *annas*.]

ALLAHABAD:
PRINTED AT THE PRESBYTERIAN MISSION PRESS.
Rev. L. G. HAY, *Superintendent*.
1853.

THE

YOGA APHORISMS

OF

PATANJALI.

BOOK II.

a. May that three-eyed Lord of the World, by whom were shown the several means for securing the difficultly attainable riches of Concentration *(yoga),* be [adjuvant] for the attainment of what is desired !*

b. Thus then having declared, in the First Book, the Concentration, along with its means, of him whose mind is abstracted [from all objects];—how, preceded by the practice of means, does the concentration of him whose mind is *not* abstracted, advance to accomplishment? [Since this question presents itself—]

---

* ते ते दुष्प्रापयोगर्द्धिसिद्धये येन दर्शिता उपायाश्च जगन्नाथस्त्र्यक्षो ऽस्तु प्रार्थिताप्तये ॥

A

in order to set forth the practice of what is instrumental thereto, he declares the practical [part of] Concentration.*

तपः स्वाध्यायेश्वरप्रणिधानानि क्रियायोगः ॥ १ ॥

Practices conducive to Concentration.

Aph. 1.—The practical [part of] Concentration is mortification *(tapas)*, muttering *(swádhyáya)*, and resignation *(pranidhána)* to the Lord.

a. The penances and fastings enjoined in another Institute [—viz. the *Dharma-śástra*—], are what are meant by 'mortification.' 'Muttering' is the muttered repetition of formulæ preceded by the mystic name of the deity [B. I. §27]. 'Resignation to the Lord' is the consigning to Him, the Supremely Venerable, without regard to fruit, all one's works. These are what are called the practical [part of] Concentration *(kriyá-yoga)*.†

b. For what purpose is this?—He replies.‡—

समाधिभावनार्थः क्लेशतनूकरणार्थश्च ॥ २ ॥

---

* तदेवं प्रथमे पादे समाहितचित्तस्य सोपायं योगमभिधाय व्युत्थितचित्तस्य कथमुपायाभ्यासपूर्वको योगस्साध्यतामुपयातीति तत्साधनानुष्ठानप्रतिपादनाय क्रियायोगमाह ॥

† तपः शास्त्रान्तरोपदिष्टं कृच्छ्रचान्द्रायणादि । स्वाध्यायः प्रणवपूर्वाणां मन्त्राणां जपः । ईश्वरप्रणिधानं सर्वक्रियाणां तस्मिन् परमगुरौ फलनिरपेक्षतया समर्पणम् । एतानि क्रियायोग इत्युच्यन्ते ॥

‡ स किमर्थ इत्यत आह ॥

The purpose of such practices.

Aph. 2.—It is for the purpose of establishing meditation, and for the purpose of extenuating afflictions.

a. The 'afflictions' *(kleśa)* will be mentioned [under §3]. The 'extenuating' of them, is the opposing their producing their effects. 'Meditation' is what has been already defined [B. I. §20, *f*]. The 'establishing' of it, is the repeatedly taking into one's thoughts [the thing to be meditated upon]. That the purpose, or motive, of which is this, is what is so called [—i. e. is what is spoken of in the aphorism].*

b. That is to say,—these, viz., penance, &c., being practised, rendering inert the 'Ignorance' and the other afflictions [§3] that assail the mind, sustain the part of subservients to Meditation. Therefore it is to the practical [part of] Concentration that the *Yogi* should first direct his attention.†

c. 'For the purpose of extenuating affiiction,'—this has been stated [in §2];—what are here meant by afflictions? He replies.‡

अविद्यास्मितारागद्वेषाभिनिवेशाः क्लेशाः ॥ ३ ॥

---

* क्लेशा वक्ष्यमाणास्तेषां तनूकरणं स्वकार्यकरणप्रतिबन्धः। समाधिरुक्तलक्षणः। तस्य भावना पुनः पुनश्चेतसि निवेशनं। सोऽर्थः प्रयोजनं यस्य तथोक्तः॥

† एतदुक्तम्भवति। एते तपःप्रभृतयोऽभ्यस्यमानाश्चित्तगतानविद्यादीन् क्लेशान् शिथिलीकुर्वन्तः समाधेरुपकारतां भजन्ते। तस्मात् प्रथमतः क्रियायोगावधारणपरेण योगिना भवितव्यमिति॥

‡ क्लेशतनूकरणार्थ इत्युक्तं। ते ऽत्र के क्लेशा इत्याह॥

Afflictions to be alleviated by such practices.

Aph. 3.—The afflictions are Ignorance, Egotism, Desire, Aversion, and Tenacity [of mundane existence].

a. And the 'afflictions,'—Ignorance and the rest,—the definitions of which will be stated [in the sequel], are five; and these, giving rise to distress, the characteristic of which is its being obstructive [to what we miserable mortals wish], are called 'afflictions,' because they, operating in the mind, consolidate that modification of the [three] Qualities which is recognised as mundane existence* [—the state of existence which it is the aim of the Yogí to eschew].

b. Although these are all equal in respect of being afflictions, yet, in order to declare that 'Ignorance' *(avidyá)*, from its being the root, is the principal one, he says.†

अविद्या क्षेत्रमुत्तरेषां प्रसुप्ततनुविच्छिन्नोदाराणाम् ॥ ४ ॥

The source of the afflictions.

Aph. 4.—Ignorance is the field of the others, whether they be dormant, extenuated, intercepted, or simple.

a. 'Ignorance' means delusion; the notion, in short, that what is *not* Soul *is* Soul. This is the 'field,'—the place of origin,

---

* क्लेशाश्चाविद्यादयो वक्ष्यमाणलक्षणाः पञ्च । ते च बाधनालक्षणं परितापमुपजनयन्तः क्लेशशब्दवाच्या भवन्ति । ते हि चेतसि प्रवर्त्तमानाः संसारलक्षणं गुणपरिणामं दृढयन्ति ॥

† सत्यपि सर्वेषां तुल्ये क्लेशत्वे मूलभूतत्वादविद्यायाः प्राधान्यं प्रतिपादयितुमाह ॥

of the others, viz., 'Egotism,' &c., which are severally fourfold through the division into 'dormant,' &c. Therefore where Ignorance, in the shape of a mistaken notion [that what is not soul is soul], becomes inoperative, there the springing up of the 'afflictions' is not seen; but, since, where this mistaken notion really exists, they *are* seen to spring up, it is quite settled that it is Ignorance that is the source.*

b. 'The dormant, extenuated, intercepted, and simple:'—among these, those 'afflictions' are called 'dormant,' which, deposited in the site of the mind, do not give rise to their effects for want of something to wake them up;—as in the state of childhood;—for the child's 'afflictions,' though present in the shape of mental deposits, are not developed for want of something to assist in awakening them.†

c. Those ['afflictions'] are the 'extenuated,' which, through one's meditating something that is opposed to each severally, their power of producing their effect having been rendered inert, abiding in the mind as a species of mental deposit, are incapable

---

* अविद्या मोहः। अनात्मन्यात्माभिमान इति यावत्। सा क्षेत्रं प्रसवभूमिरुत्तरेषामस्मितादीनां प्रत्येकं प्रसुप्तादिभेदेन चतुर्विधानां। अतो यत्राविद्या विपर्ययज्ञानरूपा शिथिलीभवति तत्र क्लेशानां नोद्भवो दृश्यते विपर्ययज्ञानसद्भावे च तेषामुद्भवदर्शनात् स्थितमेव मूलत्वमविद्यायाः॥

† प्रसुप्ततनुविच्छिन्नोदाराणामिति। तत्र ये क्लेशाश्चित्तभूमौ स्थिताः प्रबोधकाभावे स्वकार्यं नारभन्ते ते प्रसुप्ता इत्युच्यन्ते। यथा बाल्यावस्थायां। बालस्य हि वासनारूपेण स्थिता अपि क्लेशाः प्रबोधकसहकार्यभावेन न व्यज्यन्ते॥

of giving rise to their effects without an ample apparatus [of auxiliaries];—for example [such are the 'afflictions'] of the ascetic *Yogí*.*

d. Those ['afflictions'] are the 'intercepted,' which abide with their power overpowered by some strong 'affliction,'—as desire [is overpowered and 'intercepted'] when there is the condition of aversion, or aversion when there is the condition of [an overpowering] desire;—for those two, mutually opposite, cannot simultaneously co-exist.†

e. Those ['afflictions'] are the 'simple,' which operate their several effects when the things with which they co-operate are beside them;—[such are,] for example, the things adverse to Concentration at all times during the state of non-abstraction.‡

f. 'Ignorance,' though standing moreover as the *root* of these four kinds [of 'afflictions'] severally, is recognised as [also] *at*-

---

* ते तनवो ये स्वस्वप्रतिपक्षभावनया शिथिलीकृतकार्य-सम्पादनशक्तयो वासनाविशेषतया चेतस्यवस्थिताः प्रभूतां सामग्रीमन्तरेण न स्वकार्यमारब्धुं क्षमाः। यथा अभ्यास-वतो योगिनः॥

† ते विच्छिन्ना ये केनचिद्बलवता क्लेशेनाभिभूतशक्तय-स्तिष्ठन्ति। यथा द्वेषावस्थायां रागो रागावस्थायां वा द्वेषः। न ह्यनयोः परस्परविरुद्धयोर्युगपत् सम्भवोऽस्ति॥

‡ ते उदारा ये प्राप्तसहकारिसन्निधयः स्वं स्वं कार्यमभि-निर्वर्त्तयन्ति। यथा सर्वदैव योगपरिपन्थिनो व्युत्थानद-शायाम्॥

tending them; for nowhere is there found the nature of 'afflictions' having the character of being irrespective of the attendance of error; and when that, being a falsity, is removed by right knowledge, these ['afflictions'], like burnt seeds, never spring up again; hence it is ascertained that Ignorance is their cause and Ignorance is their attendant. Therefore they all partake of the name of Ignorance; and, since all the 'afflictions' cause distraction of mind, the *Yogí* must cut these off at the very outset.*

g. He defines 'Ignorance.'†

अनित्याशुचिदुःखानात्मसु नित्यशुचिसुखात्मख्यातिरविद्या ॥ ५ ॥

'Ignorance' defined.

Aph. 5.—Ignorance *(avidyá)* is the notion that the uneternal, the impure, evil, and what is not soul, are [severally] eternal, pure, joy, and soul.

---

* एषां प्रत्येकं चतुर्विधानामपि मूलभूतत्वेन स्थिताप्यविद्या अन्वयित्वेन प्रतीयते। नहि क्वचिदपि क्लेशानां विपर्ययान्वयनिरपेक्षरूपाणां स्वरूपमुपलभ्यते। तस्याञ्च मिथ्याभूतायां सम्यक् ज्ञानेन निवर्त्तितायां दग्धबीजकल्पानामेषां न क्वचित्प्ररोहो ऽस्तीति अविद्यानिमित्तत्वमविद्यान्वयश्चैषां निश्चीयते। अतः सर्वे ऽप्यविद्याव्यपदेशभाजः सर्वेषाञ्च क्लेशानां चित्तविक्षेपकारित्वाद् योगिना प्रथममेव तदुच्छेदः कर्त्तव्य इति ॥

† अविद्याया लक्षणमाह ॥

a. The definition of ignorance in general, is this,—that, ignorance is the notion that what is *not* this *is* this. The declaration of the varieties of that same [is made in the aphorism]. The notion that there is eternalness in things uneternal, such as water-jars, is called 'Ignorance.' So too the notion that things impure, such as the body, are pure; and the notion that objects which are evils are joy; and the notion that the body, which is not the soul, is the soul, [—as when a bumpkin fancies that his eye *sees*, or a phrenologist that his brain *thinks*—]. This explains the mistake of vice for virtue, and of the useless for the useful.*

b. In order to define 'Egotism', he says.†

दृग्दर्शनशक्त्योरेकात्मतेवास्मिता ॥ ६ ॥

'Egotism' defined. *Aph.* 6.—Egotism (*asmitá*) is the identifying of the power that sees with the power of seeing.

a. The 'power that sees' is Soul. The 'power of seeing' is a modification of the Quality of 'Purity' [—see Sánkhya Aphorisms, B. I. §62,] unobstructed by 'Passion' and 'Darkness', in the shape of the internal organ [or Mind]. What is called

---

* अतस्मिन् तत्प्रतिभासो ऽविद्येत्यविद्यायाः सामान्यलक्षणं। तस्या एव भेदप्रतिपादनं। अनित्येषु घटादिषु नित्यत्वाभिमानो ऽविद्येत्युच्यते। एवमशुचिषु कायादिषु शुचित्वाभिमानो दुःखेषु च विषयेषु सुखत्वाभिमानो ऽनात्मनि शरीरे आत्मत्वाभिमानः। एतेन अपुण्ये पुण्यभ्रमो ऽनर्थे चार्थभ्रमो व्याख्यातः ॥

† अस्मितां लक्षयितुमाह ॥

'Egotism' is the notion that these two things, entirely different as being the experienced and the experiencer—the unintelligent and the *not* unintelligent,—are one and the same. For example,—Nature, though really neither agent nor experiencer, fancies "*I* am agent,—*I* am experiencer":—this blunder is the 'affliction' called 'Egotism.'*

b. He states the definition of 'Desire' *(rága)*.†

सुखानुशयी रागः॥ ७॥

Desire defined.

Aph. 7.—Desire is what dwells on pleasure.

a. 'Dwells on pleasure'—i. e. reposes on [—or is the affection of the mind when the thought rests on—] joy. This 'affliction', named 'Desire,' is a longing, in the shape of a thirst, for the means of enjoyment, preceded by [—or, in other words, consequent on] the remembrance of enjoyment, on the part of him who has known joy.‡

b. He states the definition of 'Aversion' *(dwesha)*.§

---

* दृक्शक्तिः पुरुषः। दर्शनशक्ती रजस्तमोभ्यामनभिभूतः सात्त्विकः परिणामोऽन्तकरणरूपः। तयोर्भोग्यभोक्तृत्वेन जडाजडत्वेनचात्यन्तं भिन्नयोरेकताभिमानोऽस्मितेत्युच्यते। यथा। प्रकृतिर्वस्तुतः कर्तृत्वभोक्तृत्वरहितापि कर्त्र्यहं भोक्त्र्यहमित्यभिमन्यते सोऽयमस्मिताख्यो विपर्यासः क्लेशः॥

† रागस्य लक्षणमाह॥

‡ सुखमनुशेते इति सुखानुशयी। सुखज्ञस्य सुखानुस्मृतिपूर्वकः सुखसाधनेषु तृष्णारूपो गर्द्धो रागसञ्ज्ञः क्लेशः॥

§ द्वेषस्य लक्षणमाह॥

B

दुःखानुशयी द्वेषः ॥ ८ ॥

Aversion defined.

Aph. 8.—Aversion is what dwells on pain.

a. 'Pain' is what has been already defined [—B. I. §31. *b*]. Of him who has known it, disliking what things occasion it, in consequence of his remembrance of it, the feeling of disapproval is the 'affliction' called 'aversion'.*

b. He states what is 'tenacity of life'† *(abhinives'a)*.

स्वरसवाही विदुषो ऽपि तन्वनुबन्धो ऽभिनिवेशः ॥ ९ ॥

The clinging to mundane existence.

Aph. 9.—Continuant through its self-reproductive property, even on the part of the wise, attachment to the body is 'Tenacity of life.'

a. Continuant 'through its self-reproductive property;'—that is to say, it flows on by reason of its own nature, just by reason of its being self-continuant. The 'affliction' called 'tenacity of life' is what prevails in the case of every one, from the worm up to Brahmá, without any concomitant cause [in addition to its own self-continuant property], in the shape of the constant clinging [which expresses itself in such terms as], "May I not be separated from the body and things sensible, &c.,"—this springing up in the shape of dread, through the force of the im-

* दुःखमुक्तलक्षणं। तदभिज्ञस्य तदनुस्मृतिपूर्वकं तत्साधनेषु अनभिलषतो यो ऽयं निन्दात्मकः स द्वेषलक्षणः क्लेशः ॥

† अभिनिवेशमाह ॥

pression from the experience of the pain of a death that took place in a previous life.*

b. Since thus, then, non-abstraction is made up of the 'afflictions,' the 'afflictions' are at the outset to be removed by the practice of intentness on a single point;—such is the import.†

c. And not without their being known can these be removed; therefore having, with a view to the knowledge of them, declared their name, source, division, and characteristic, he now states the division of the methods for the removal of these bipartitely gross and subtile‡.

ते प्रतिप्रसवहेयाः सूक्ष्माः ॥ १० ॥

The Subtile 'afflictions' how to be evaded.

Aph. 10.—These, when subtile, are to be evaded by an antagonistic production.

---

* स्वस्य रसेन संस्कारेणैव वहतीति स्वरसवाही । पूर्वजन्मजातमरणदुःखानुभववासनाबलात् भयरूपः समुपजायमानः शरीरविषयादिभिर्मम वियोगो मा भूदित्यन्वहमनवच्छिन्नरूपः सर्वस्यैवाक्रमेर्ब्रह्मपर्यन्तं निमित्तं विना प्रवर्त्तमानो ऽभिनिवेशाख्यः क्लेशः ॥

† तदेवं व्युत्थानस्य क्लेशात्मकत्वाद् एकाग्रताभ्यासेन प्रथमं क्लेशाः परिहर्त्तव्या इत्याशयः ॥

‡ नचाज्ञातानां तेषां परिहारः शक्यः कर्त्तुमिति तज्ज्ञानाय तेषामुद्देशं क्षेत्रं विभागं लक्षणमभिधाय स्थूलसूक्ष्मभेदभिन्नानां तेषां प्रहाणोपायविभागमाह ॥

a. These subtile 'afflictions,' which, abiding in the form of mental deposits, do not occasion any change, in the shape of a 'modification' [—see B. 1. §5,—stored in the mind, like Locke's 'ideas' while not objects of attention—], these are 'to be evaded,' to be avoided, 'by an antagonistic production,' by an alteration adverse to them. When the understanding, with its deposits, having done its work, lapses into its cause, viz., egotism, then how should these ['afflictions'], being deprived of their root, possibly continue?*

b. He now mentions the method for the removal of the 'gross' ones.†

ध्यानहेयास्तद्वृत्तयः ॥ ११ ॥

The gross 'afflictions' how to be got rid of.

Aph. 11.—Their 'modifications' [—when the 'afflictions' modify the mind by pressing themselves upon the attention—] are to be got rid of by meditation.

a. The 'modifications,' in the shape of pleasure, pain, or indifference, which consist of these 'afflictions' that have set in operation their effects,—*these* are 'to be got rid of,' to be quitted, by means of meditation, i. e., by intentness of the mind on a single point;—such is the meaning.‡

---

* ते सूक्ष्माः क्लेशा ये वासनारूपेणावस्थिता न वृत्तिरूपं परिणाममारभन्ते ते प्रतिप्रसवेन प्रतिलोमपरिणामेन हेयास्त्यक्तव्याः । स्वकारणास्मितायां कृतार्थं सवासनं चित्तं यदा प्रविष्टं भवति तदा कुतस्तेषां निर्मूलकानां सम्भवः ॥

† स्थूलानां हानोपायमाह ॥

‡ तेषां क्लेशानामारब्धकार्याणां याः सुखदुःखमोहा-

b. These 'from their being gross, can be removed by the mere practice of what purifies the mind [—see B. I. §33, *c*—], as the coarse gross dirt on clothes and the like is removed by mere washing; but that subtile [impurity] which is in them can be removed only by such [more recondite] expedients as bleaching, &c.*

c. Having thus mentioned what the 'afflictions' are he remarks as follows, with the view of mentioning the stock of works† [that stands at each man's credit or discredit].

क्लेशमूलः कर्माशयो दृष्टादृष्टजन्मवेदनीयः ॥ १२ ॥

One's merits and demerits.

Aph. 12.—The stock of works, whose root is the 'afflictions,' is what is to be had fruition of in this visible state, or in that unseen.

a. By 'the stock of works' the nature of this [that he is speaking of] is set forth, for works exist only in the shape of mental deposits.‡

त्मिका वृत्तयः ता ध्यानेन चित्तैकाग्रतालक्षणेन हेया हातव्या इत्यर्थः ॥

* चित्तपरिकर्माभ्यासमात्रेणैव स्थूलत्वात्तासां निवृत्तिर्भवति यथा वस्त्रादौ घनः स्थूलो मलः प्रक्षालनमात्रेणैव निवर्त्तते यस्तु तत्र सूक्ष्मः स तैस्तैरुपायैरुत्तापनप्रभृतिभिरेव निवर्त्तयितुं शक्यते ॥

† एवं क्लेशानां तत्त्वमभिधाय कर्माशयस्याभिधातुमाह ॥

‡ कर्माशय इत्यनेन तस्य स्वरूपमभिहितं यतो वासनारूपाण्येव कर्माणि ॥

b. By 'whose root is the afflictions' the *cause* is set forth, since the 'afflictions' alone are the cause of acts.*

c. By 'what is to be had fruition of in this visible state, or in that unseen,' the fruit is declared. What is to be experienced in this present state, is 'what is to be had fruition of in this visible state.' What is to be experienced in another life, is 'what is to be had fruition of in that unseen.'†

d. Thus some meritorious acts, such as the worship of the gods, performed with excessive impetuosity [—see B. I. §21, *b*—], bestow, even in this life, fruit in the shape of rank, years, and enjoyment,—as distinguished rank [—that of a demigod—], &c., accrued, even in this life, to Nandíśwara, through the force of his worship of the divine Maheśwara. So to others, as Viśwamitra [—who, according to the *Rámáyaṇa*, from being a *Kshattriya* was raised to the rank of a *Bráhmaṇ*—], through the efficacy of penance, rank and long life [have accrued]. To others [has accrued change of] rank only,—as the change to another rank, &c., of those doing wicked acts with hot impetuosity, such as Nahusha [who was changed to a snake], and Urvaśí [—the nymph who was punished] by her metamorphosis into a creeper in the grove of Kártikeya. In this way is the rule to be applied, according to circumstances, distributively or collectively,‡

---

* क्लेशमूल इत्यनेन कारणमभिहितं यतः कर्म्मणां क्लेशा एव निमित्तम्॥

† दृष्टादृष्टवेदनीय इत्यनेन फलमुक्तम्। अस्मिन्नेव जन्मनि अनुभवनीयो दृष्टजन्मवेदनीयः। जन्मान्तरानुभवनीयो ऽदृष्टवेदनीयः॥

‡ तथाहि कानिचित्पुण्यानि कर्म्माणि देवताराधनादीनि तीव्रसंवेगेन कृतानीहैव जन्मनि फलं जात्यायुर्भोग-

[—each well-deserving or ill-deserving person being understood to receive rank, or years, or enjoyment, one or more of them, or all of them, or none of them,—and so on through the string of permutations and combinations possible].

e. Now he mentions the fruit of the stock of works divided according to its division* [into merit and demerit].

सति मूले तद्विपाको जात्यायुर्भोगः ॥ १३ ॥

The fruit of works. *Aph.* 13—While there is the root, its fructification is rank, years, and enjoyment.

a. The 'afflictions' above-mentioned are the 'root;' whilst these remain unsubdued, of these acts, virtuous or vicious, 'rank, years, and enjoyment,' are the 'fructification,' i. e. the fruit. 'Rank' means the being a man [or a god, or a beast,] or the like. 'Years' mean abiding for a long time in the body. 'Enjoyments' mean sense-objects, the senses, and the aggregate of pleasures and pains, because the word *bhoga* [—here rendered 'enjoyment'—] is formed [from the root *bhuj*] so as to denote the object, the instrument, or the state† [of enjoyment].

लक्षणां प्रयच्छन्ति यथा नन्दीश्वरस्य भगवन्महेश्वराराधनबलादिहैव जन्मनि जात्यादयो विशिष्टाः प्रादुर्भूताः । एवमन्येषां विश्वामित्रादीनां तपःप्रभावाज्जात्यायुषी । केषाञ्चिज्जातिरेव । यथा तीव्रसंवेगेन दुष्टकर्मकृतां नहुषादीनां जात्यन्तरादिपरिणाम उर्वश्याश्च कार्त्तिकेयवने लतारूपतया । एवं व्यस्तसमस्तरूपत्वेन यथायोगं योज्यम् ॥

* इदानीं कर्माशयस्य स्वभेदभिन्नं फलमाह ॥

† मूलमुक्तलक्षणाः क्लेशाः । तेष्वनभिभूतेषु सत्सु तेषां

b. The gist of this is this, that the mental deposits of works, collected, from time without beginning, in the ground of the mind, as they by degrees arrive at maturation, so do they, existing in lesser or greater measure [—the sum of the merit being lesser than that of the demerit, or conversely—], lead to their effects in the shape of rank [raised or lowered—], years, and enjoyment* [or experience of good or ill].

c. In respect of the 'rank,' &c., that have been declared to be the fruit of acts, he states, according to the works that are the cause of each, which is the efficient of which effect.†

ते ह्लादपरितापफलाः पुण्यापुण्यहेतुत्वात्॥ १४ ॥

What works have what fruits.

Aph. 14.—These have joy or suffering as their fruits, accordingly as the cause is virtue or vice.

a. 'Joy' means pleasure; 'suffering' means pain. Those the fruit of which are joy and suffering, are what are so named [—i.

कर्मणां कुशलाकुशलरूपाणां विपाकः फलं जात्यायुर्भोगा भवन्ति। जातिर्मनुष्यत्वादिः। आयुश्चिरकालं कायसम्बन्धः। भोगा विषया इन्द्रियाणि सुखदुःखसंविच्च कर्मकरणभावसाधनव्युत्पत्त्या भोगशब्दस्य॥

* इदमत्र तात्पर्यं चित्तभूमावनादिकालसञ्चिताः कर्मवासना यथा यथा पाकमुपयान्ति तथा तथा गुणप्रधानभावेन स्थिता जात्यायुर्भोगलक्षणं स्वकार्यमारभन्ते॥

† उक्तानां कर्मफलत्वेन जात्यादीनां स्वकारणकर्मानुसारेण कार्यकर्तृत्वमाह॥

e. are what are denoted in the aphorism by the compound term here analysed]. By 'virtue' (*punya*) is meant any good deed; by 'vice,' its opposite. Of what things these two, viz., virtue and vice, are the causes, the nature of these things [is what is meant by the compound term *punyápunyahetukatwa*; and it is] thereby* [—or accordingly as the cause is virtue or vice, that the effect is joy or suffering].

b. What is asserted is this, that the rank, years, and enjoyment, originating in good works, are pleasant fruits; and what originate in evil acts are painful fruits.†

c. This twofold character [of the fruit of works] is in respect of mortals simply; but to the Yogí *all* [mundane experience] is sorrow, as he proceeds to state.‡

परिणामतापसंस्कारदुःखैर्गुणवृत्तिविरोधाच्च दुःखमेव सर्वं विवेकिनः ॥ १५ ॥

Pleasure and pain alike vexations to the Yogí.

Aph. 15.—And, to the discriminating, *all* is grief simply, since the modifications due to the Qualities are adverse [to the summum bonum] through

---

* ह्लादः सुखं। परितापो दुःखं। ह्लादपरितापौ फलं येषां ते तथोक्ताः। पुण्यं कुशलं कर्म। तद्विपरीतमपुण्यं। ते पुण्यापुण्ये कारणे येषां तेषां भावस्तस्मात् ॥

† एतदुक्तम्भवति पुण्यकर्मारब्धजात्यायुर्भोगा ह्लादफलाः। अपुण्यारब्धाः परितापफलाः ॥

‡ एतच्च प्राणिमात्रापेक्षया द्वैविध्यं योगिनस्तु सर्वं दुःखमित्याह ॥

C

the vexations of the various forms [of Nature], and of anxiety and of impressions self-continuant.

a. That is to say,—[in the opinion] of him who understands discriminatively the 'affections,' &c., *every* instrument of experience [whether of pleasure or of pain] that comes under his view, is, like food with poison in it, a grief only,—something felt to be against the grain.*

b. Since the Yogí who has become a complete adept is distressed even by the slightest pain,—as the eye-ball, and no other member, experiences great pain from the mere touch of a thread of wool, so the discriminating [votary of Quietude] is averse to the adherence of even a very little pain;—*how* is it [that he shrinks from such pains]? To this he replies, 'through the vexations of the various forms, and of anxiety, and of impressions self-continuant.†

c. Since there is increase of desire in proportion as more objects are enjoyed, and since these [objects] are causes of other pains occasioned by their non-attainment, they are really nothing else than griefs [—according to the principle that the nature of the cause is not other than the nature of the product—]; thus

---

* परिज्ञातक्लेशादिविवेकस्य परिदृश्यमानं सकलमेव भोगसाधनं सविषान्नवत् दुःखमेव प्रतिकूलवेदनीयमित्यर्थः ॥

† यस्मादत्यन्ताभिजातो योगी दुःखलेशेनाप्युद्विजते यथाक्षिपात्रमूर्णातन्तुस्पर्शमात्रेणैव महतीं पीडामनुभवति नेतरदङ्गं तथा विवेकी स्वल्पदुःखानुषङ्गेनापि विरज्यते। कथमित्याह परिणामतापसंस्कारदुःखैः ॥

is it that the various forms [of Nature presented to us in the shape of objects] are sorrow.*

d. While the means of enjoyment are being enjoyed, since there must ever exist an aversion towards what is hostile to that [enjoyment,—so that thus ever "surgit amari aliquid medio de fonte leporum"—], even at the time of experiencing pleasure, the pain of distress is hard to be got rid of,—such is what constitutes the pain [called] anxiety.†

e. As for the fact that 'impressions self-continuant' are griefs, —the sense of enjoyment, and the sense of suffering, that arises on the contact of objects which one desires or does not desire, originates in one's [mental] field a corresponding self-continuant impression. Again we [thence] experience sensations of the same sort, so that, since, through the emergence of innumerable self-continuant impressions, the mundane state is never cut short, every-thing whatever is a grief.‡

---

* विषयाणामुपभुज्यमानानां यथायथं गर्द्धाभिवृद्धेस्तद्प्राप्तिकृतस्य दुःखान्तरसाधनत्वाच्चास्त्येव दुःखरूपतेति परिणामदुःखत्वम् ॥

† उपभुज्यमानेषु सुखसाधनेषु तत्प्रतिपन्थिनं प्रति द्वेषस्य सर्वदैवावस्थितत्वात् सुखानुभवकालेऽपि तापदुःखं दुष्परिहारमिति तापदुःखता ॥

‡ संस्कारदुःखत्वं । स्वाभिमतानभिमतविषयसन्निधाने सुखसंविद्दुःखसंविच्चोपजायमाना तथाविधमेव स्वक्षेत्रे संस्कारमारभते । पुनस्तथाविधसंविदनुभव इत्यपरिमितसंस्कारोत्पत्तिद्वारेण संसारानुच्छेदात्सर्वस्यैव दुःखत्वम् ॥

f. 'And since the modifications due to the Qualities are adverse.' Of the Qualities, viz., Purity, Passion, and Darkness, the modifications [or psychical influences] which arise in the shape of Pleasure, Pain, and Indifference, are opposed to one another, since they reciprocally are overpowered or do overpower. These are but griefs, since they are, in absolutely every instance, the cause of grief* [—grief continuing while the mundane state due to the Qualities continues].

g. What is asserted is this, that to the discriminating one, who desires entire and complete cessation of suffering, the whole quaternion [enumerated in the aphorism] are causes of the alleged description† [i. e., causes of grief]. Hence, since all objects exhibit themselves in the shape of vexations, therefore the harvest of all works is in the shape of vexation alone.†

h. This, that, since the aforesaid fund of 'afflictions', the harvest of [each one's] stock of works, takes its rise in Ignorance, and since Ignorance, as being in the shape of false knowledge, is to be expelled by correct knowledge, and since correct knowledge consists in the ascertainment of what is to be rejected and what to be accepted, with the means [of rejection, &c.,]—in order [—I repeat—] to declare this, he says.‡—

* गुणवृत्तिविरोधाच्चेति। गुणानां सत्त्वरजस्तमसां या वृत्तयः सुखदुःखमोहरूपाः परस्परमभिभाव्याभिभावकत्वेन विरुद्धा जायन्ते। तासां सर्वत्रैव दुःखानुबन्धाद् दुःखत्वं॥

† एतदुक्तम्भवति। ऐकान्तिकीमात्यन्तिकीञ्च दुःखनिवृत्तिमिच्छतो विवेकिन उक्तरूपकारणं चतुष्टयं। यावत्सर्वे विषया दुःखस्वरूपतया प्रतिभान्ति तस्मात्सर्वकर्मविपाको दुःखरूप एवेति॥

‡ एतदेवमुक्तस्य क्लेशकर्माशयविपाकराशेरविद्याप्रभव-

हेयं दुःखमनागतम् ॥ १६ ॥

What is to be shunned.

Aph. 16.—What is to be shunned is pain not yet come.

a. Since what *has* been is past, and what is *being* experienced is incapable of being shunned [*whilst* being experienced], it is only mundane pain not yet arrived that is to be shunned :—such is what is here asserted.*

b. He states the cause of that which is to be shunned.†

द्रष्टृदृश्ययोः संयोगो हेयहेतुः ॥ १७ ॥

The origin of evil.

Aph. 17.—The cause of what is to be shunned is the conjunction of the seer with the visual.

a. The 'seer'—in the shape of Thought. The 'visual' means the principle of understanding [which does not itself see, but is Thought's organ]. The conjunction of these two, occasioned by the absence of discriminative knowledge,—their contact as the experienced [—for all that seems external is developed out of the principle of the understanding—] and the experiencer, —*this* is the cause or reason 'of what is to be shunned,'—of

---

त्वादविद्यायाश्च मिथ्याज्ञानरूपतया सम्यग्ज्ञानोच्छेद्यत्वात्सम्यग्ज्ञानस्य ससाधनहेयोपादेयावधारणरूपत्वात् तदभिधानायाह ॥

* भूतस्य व्यतिक्रान्तत्वादनुभूयमानस्य च त्यक्तुमशक्यत्वादनागतमेव संसारदुःखं हातव्यमित्युक्तमिति ॥

† हेयहेतुमाह ॥

pain,—of the world in the shape of a modification of the Qualities;—because when *this* surceases, the mundane state surceases,—such is the meaning.*

a. We have spoken of 'the conjunction of the seer with the visual.' Among these things, of the 'visual' he states the nature, the products, and the motive.†

प्रकाशक्रियास्थितिशीलम्भूतेन्द्रियात्मकं भोगापवर्गार्थं दृश्यम् ॥ १८ ॥

The nature and purpose of the visible.

Aph. 18.—The visual [—including the visible—] whose habit is illumination, action, and rest, and which consists of the Elements and the Organs, is for the sake of experience and emancipation.

a. 'Illumination' is the property of 'Purity'. 'Action,' in the shape of exertion, is that of 'Passion.' 'Rest,' in the shape of fixation, is that of 'Darkness.' Of which these,—illumination, action, and rest,—are the habit, or the essential nature,—*that* is what is so described [—i. e. described in the aphorism by the compound epithet here analysed]. Thus has its nature been set forth.‡

---

* द्रष्टा चिद्रूपः। दृश्यं बुद्धितत्त्वं। तयोरविवेकख्यातिपूर्वको यो ऽसौ संयोगो भोग्यभोक्तृत्वेन सन्निधानं स हेयस्य दुःखस्य गुणपरिणामरूपस्य संसारस्य हेतुः कारणं। तन्निवृत्त्या संसारनिवृत्तिर्भवतीत्यर्थः॥

† द्रष्टृदृश्ययोः संयोग इत्युक्तं। तत्र दृश्यस्य स्वरूपं कार्यं प्रयोजनञ्चाह॥

‡ प्रकाशः सत्त्वस्य धर्मः। क्रिया प्रवृत्तिरूपा रजसः।

b. 'Consisting of the Elements and the Organs.' The 'Elements,' according to their division into the Gross and the Subtile, are Earth, &c., and the rudiments of Odour; &c. The 'Organs,' according to their division into the organs of knowing, the organs of action, and the internal organ, are of three sorts. Of which this two-fold character of percept and perception is 'what it consists of,'—a modification not other than itself,—*that* is what is so described [—i. e. described as 'consisting of the Elements and the Organs']. Thus have its products [—which are not other than Nature herself—] been stated.*

c. 'Experience' means what has been already defined [at §13. *a*]. 'Emancipation' is the surcease, occasioned by discriminative knowledge, of the mundane state. Of which these two, experience and emancipation, are the motive or purpose, *that* is what is so described [—i. e. described by the compound epithet now analysed—], that is to say 'the visual [including the visible.]'†

स्थितिर्नियमरूपा तमसः। ताः प्रकाशक्रियास्थितयः शीलं स्वाभाविकं रूपं यस्य तत्तथाविधमिति स्वरूपमस्य निर्दिष्टम्॥

* भूतेन्द्रियात्मकमिति। भूतानि स्थूलसूक्ष्मभेदेन पृथिव्यादीनि गन्धतन्मात्राणि च। इन्द्रियाणि बुद्धीन्द्रियकर्मेन्द्रियान्तःकरणभेदेन त्रिविधानि। उभयमेतद्ग्राह्यग्रहणरूपमात्मा स्वरूपाभिन्नः परिणामो यस्य तत्तथाविधमित्यनेन कार्यमस्योक्तम्॥

† भोगः कथितलक्षणः। अपवर्गो विवेकख्यातिपूर्विका संसारनिवृत्तिः। तौ भोगापवर्गावर्थः प्रयोजनं यस्य तत्तथाविधं दृश्यमित्यर्थः॥

d. And since this, the 'visible,' which consists of modifications in the shape of various conditions, requires to be known as what is to be shunned in order to declare its conditions, he says.*

विशेषाविशेषलिङ्गमात्रालिङ्गानि गुणपर्वाणि ॥ १९ ॥

The aspects of the Qualities.

Aph. 19.—The divisions [of condition] of the Qualities are (1) the diverse, (2) the non-diverse, (3) the merely [once] resolvable, and (4) the irresolvable.

a. The divisions, i. e. the several conditions, of the Qualities are to be understood to be four,—such is what we are here informed of. Among these, the 'diverse' are the gross elements and the organs; the 'non-diverse' are the subtile elements and the internal organ; the 'merely [once] resolvable' is intellect [—which is resolvable into the Undiscrete, but not further—]; the 'irresolvable' is the Undiscrete [or Nature] :—thus has it been declared.†

b. The four conditions [of developement] of the Qualities are set forth as necessarily requiring to be known at the time of Concentration, because we recognise the Undiscrete, which consists of the three Qualities, as being present everywhere that

---

* तस्यच दृश्यस्य नानावस्थारूपपरिणामात्मकस्य हेयत्वेन ज्ञातव्यत्वादवस्थाः कथयितुमाह ॥

† गुणानां पर्वाण्यवस्थाविशेषाश्चत्वारो ज्ञातव्या इत्युपदिष्टम्भवति। तत्र विशेषा महाभूतेन्द्रियाणि। अविशेषास्तन्मात्रान्तःकरणे। लिङ्गमात्रं बुद्धिः। अलिङ्गमव्यक्तमित्युक्तम् ॥

these are,* [—so that if we did not know these, then the Undiscrete, the cause of bondage, might be present undetected].

c. Since the visible requires first to be known as that which is to be shunned, having thus explained it, with its conditions, in order now to explain what is to be accepted [and not to be got rid of—viz.] the 'seer,'—he says.†

द्रष्टा दृशिमात्रः शुद्धोऽपि प्रत्ययानुपश्यः ॥ २० ॥

Soul defined.

Aph. 20.—The 'seer' [Soul] is vision simply, though pure, looking directly on ideas.

a. The 'seer,' i. e., Soul, is 'vision simply,' i. e., mere Thought. This 'though pure,' i. e. though abiding as itself, without becoming modified, or the like. 'Looking directly on ideas:'—'ideas' are thought coloured by objects:—it looks 'directly on' these,—immediately,—without the intervention of successive stages, or the like. What is asserted is this, that, whilst it is only the intellect that becomes coloured by the object, Soul is spectator merely through proximity.‡

---

* सर्वत्र त्रिगुणरूपस्याव्यक्तस्यान्वयित्वेन प्रत्यभिज्ञानादवश्यं ज्ञातव्यत्वेन योगकाले चत्वारि पर्वाणि निर्दिष्टानि ॥

† एवं हेयत्वेन दृश्यस्य प्रथमं ज्ञातव्यत्वात्तदवस्थासहितं व्याख्यायोपादेयं द्रष्टारं व्याकर्त्तुमाह ॥

‡ द्रष्टा पुरुषो दृशिमात्रश्चेतनमात्रः । स शुद्धोऽपि । परिणामित्वाद्यभावेन स्वप्रतिष्ठोऽपि । प्रत्ययानुपश्यः । प्रत्यया विषयोपरक्तानि ज्ञानानि । तानि अनु अव्यवधानेन प्रतिसङ्क्रमाद्यभावेन पश्यति । एतदुक्तम्भवति । जातविषयोपरागायामेव बुद्धौ सन्निधानमात्रेणैव पुरुषस्य द्रष्टृत्वमिति ॥

b. It alone is the experiencer ;—so he says.*—

तदर्थ एव दृश्यात्मा ॥ २१ ॥

Soul is the experiencer.

Aph. 21.—For the sake of it alone is the entity of the visible.

a. The 'entity,' the self, of the 'visible' which has been already defined [§17. *a.*],—this is 'for the sake of *it*;'—the bringing about that '*it*,' the Soul, shall be an experiencer, is its aim, to the exclusion in short of any selfish end. For Nature, energizing, energizes not with a view to any purpose of her own, but with the design "Let me bring about Soul's experience."†

b. If thus the motive be only the effecting of Soul's experience, then, when this has been effected, it should cease striving for that in the absence of a motive :—and, when it is free from alteration, since it is pure [—exhibiting neither the Qualities of Passion nor of Darkness when all three are in calm equipoise—], all souls should be freed from bondage, and the mundane state should be cut short. Having pondered this doubt, he says‡—

---

* स एव भोक्तेत्यत आह ॥

† दृश्यस्य प्रागुक्तलक्षणस्य आत्मा यत्स्वरूपं स तदर्थस्तस्य पुरुषस्य भोक्तृत्वसम्पादनं नाम स्वार्थपरिहारेण प्रयोजनं। नहि प्रधानं प्रवर्त्तमानमात्मनः किञ्चित्प्रयोजनमपेक्ष्य प्रवर्त्तते किन्तु पुरुषस्य भोगं सम्पादयामीति ॥

‡ यद्येवं पुरुषस्य भोगसम्पादनमेव प्रयोजनं तदा सम्पादिते तस्मिंस्तस्मिन्निष्प्रयोजनं विरतव्यापारं स्यात्। तस्मिंश्च परिणामशून्ये शुद्धत्वात् सर्वे द्रष्टारो बन्धरहिताः स्युस्ततस्संसारोच्छेद इत्याशंक्याह ॥

कृतार्थं प्रति नष्टमप्यनष्टं तदन्यसाधारणत्वात् ॥ २२ ॥

The emancipation of one entails not that of others.

Aph. 22.—Though it have ceased to be, in respect of him who has effected what is required, it has not ceased [in regard to all], because it is common to others besides him.

a. Although, since it causes experience just till there is discriminative knowledge, it ceases to be, i. e., desists from acting, in respect of some soul which has effected the end [of discerning discriminatively], still, since it is common to all souls, it continues, as regards others, with its operations undestroyed. Therefore, since Nature is common to all experiencers, it never ceases; nor does the emancipation of one involve the emancipation of all:—such is what is asserted.*

b. Having explained the 'visible' and the 'seer,' in order to explain their conjunction, he says—‡

स्वस्वामिशक्त्योः स्वरूपोपलब्धिहेतुः संयोगः ॥ २३ ॥

The conjunction of soul and nature what.

Aph. 23.—The conjunction is the cause of the apprehension of the actual condition of the natures of the possessed and the possessor.

---

* यद्यपि विवेकख्यातिपर्यन्ताद्भोगसम्पादनात्कमपि कृतार्थं पुरुषं प्रति तन्नष्टं विरतव्यापारं तथापि सर्वपुरुषसाधारणत्वादन्यान् प्रत्यनष्टव्यापारमवतिष्ठते। अतः प्रधानस्य सकलभोक्तृसाधारणत्वान्न कदाचनापि विनाश एकस्य मुक्तौ वा न सर्वेषां मुक्तिप्रसङ्ग इत्युक्तम्भवति ॥

† दृश्यद्रष्टारौ व्याख्याय संयोगं व्याख्यातुमाह ॥

a. He characterises this through its effect* [—telling us not what the conjunction is, but what it is the cause of].

b. 'The nature of the possessed' is the nature of the visible. 'The nature of the possessor' is the nature of the 'seer.' Moreover, the apprehension of the nature of these two, correlated as the known and the knower,—that which is the cause of *this* is the conjunction [here spoken of];—and this is none other than the nature of their cognate habit as the experienced and the experiencer. Because, of these two, which are from everlasting and all-pervading, there is no conjunction other than their essential character. That the experienced's character as something experienced, and the experiencer's character as an experiencer, has existed from everlasting,—this alone is the conjunction† [or relation between the two].

c. Moreover he states the cause thereof.‡

तस्य हेतुर्हेयमविद्या ॥ २४ ॥

The cause of the conjunction.

Aph. 24.—The cause thereof is what is to be quitted—viz., Ignorance.

---

* कार्यद्वारेणास्य लक्षणं करोति ॥

† स्वशक्तिर्दृश्यस्य स्वभावः। स्वामिशक्तिर्द्रष्टुः स्वरूपं। तयोर्द्वयोरपि संवेद्यसंवेदकत्वेन व्यवस्थितयोर्या स्वरूपोपलब्धिस्तस्याः कारणं यस्संयोगः। सच सहजभोग्यभोक्तृभावस्वरूपान्नान्यः। नहि तयोर्नित्ययोर्व्यापकयोश्च स्वरूपादतिरिक्तः कश्चित्संयोगः। यदेव भोग्यस्य भोग्यत्वं भोक्तुश्च भोक्तृत्वमनादिसिद्धं स एव संयोगः॥

‡ तस्यापि कारणमाह॥

a. That which has been already described [§4.] as Ignorance, in the shape of delusion, consisting in the confounding the unreal with the real, is declared to be of that conjunction in the shape of the absence of discriminative knowledge, the cause,—what is to quitted,—the [grammatical] object of the act of 'quitting.'*

b. What, again, is the 'quitting' thereof? To this he replies.†

तदभावात्संयोगाभावो हानं तद्दृशेः कैवल्यम् ॥ २५ ॥

The quitting of conjunction what.

Aph. 25.—The 'quitting' consists in the surcease of the conjunction, on that [Ignorance];—*this* is the isolation of the soul.

a. 'Of that,' i. e., of Ignorance, eradicated by its essential opposite, viz., right knowledge, 'the surcease,'—when this takes place, the surcease also of its effect, viz., of the conjunction, is what is called the 'quitting' of it.‡

b. What is meant is as follows;—abandonment does not apply in the case of this as in that of a circumscribed body [from which you may disjoin yourself by moving away into a portion of space unoccupied by it]; but, when discriminative knowledge

---

* या पूर्वं विपर्य्यासात्मिका मोहरूपा ऽविद्या व्याख्याता सा तस्या ऽविवेकख्यातिरूपस्य संयोगस्य कारणं हेयं हानक्रियाकर्मोच्यते ॥

† किम्पुनस्तद्धानमित्याह ॥

‡ तस्या अविद्यायाः स्वरूपविरुद्धेन सम्यग् ज्ञानेनोन्मूलितायाया यो ऽयमभावस्तस्मिन् सति तत्कार्यस्य संयोगस्याप्यभावस्तद्धानमित्युच्यते ॥

has been produced, the conjunction, which was due to the absence of discriminative knowledge, ceases quite of its own accord;—such is the 'quitting' of it. And, moreover, that quitting which there is of conjunction [with Nature], being for all eternity, is what is called the isolation *(kaivalya)* of the soul [thereafter existing entirely] *alone (kewala)*.*

c. Thus have the nature, the cause, and the effect, of the conjunction [of soul with Nature] been declared.†

d. Now, by means of declaring the means of 'quitting' [what ought to be quitted], he states [by implication] the cause of [the attainment of] what [condition] ought to be accepted‡ [as the most desirable possible].

विवेकख्यातिरविप्लवा हानोपायः ॥ २६ ॥

The means of quitting the conjunction.

Aph. 26.—The means of quitting [the state of bondage] is discriminative knowledge not discontinuous.

a. The 'knowledge,'—the perfect cognizance, of the distinction, in this shape, viz., that the Qualities are one thing and Soul is another thing, is 'the means,' the cause, 'of quitting,' i. e., of abandoning, the visible [or phenomenal]. *What* sort of [knowledge]? 'Not discontinuous.' That [knowledge] is 'not discontinuous,' in respect of which there is no skipping,—no

* अयमर्थो नैतस्य मूर्त्तद्रव्यवत् परित्यागो युज्यते किन्तु जातायां विवेकख्यातावविवेकख्यातिनिमित्तसंयोगः स्वयमेव निवर्त्तत इति तस्य हानं। यदेवच संयोगस्य हानं तदेव नित्यं केवलस्यापि पुरुषस्य कैवल्यं व्यपदिश्यते ॥

† तदेवं संयोगस्य स्वरूपं कारणं कार्यञ्चाभिहितम् ॥

‡ अथ हानोपायकथनद्वारेणोपादेयकारणमाह ॥

breaks between and between, in the shape of non-abstraction* [or re-conjunction of soul with the things of sense].

b. The import here is this, that, when Ignorance is dissolved by force of meditating on what is opposed to it, that advent which there is of a reflection, in the soul, of the introspective intellect, where the conceit of being knower or agent has been laid aside, and when it is unoppressed by the filth of Passion and Darkness, is what is called discriminative knowledge, [—or the knowledge of the non-identity of soul and Nature]. And when this prevails permanently, there simply becomes, through the cessation of the rule of the visible, *isolation*.†

c. While telling of what description is the discernment of that soul in which discriminative knowledge has taken place, he declares [by implication] the nature of discriminative knowledge itself.‡

---

* अन्ये गुणा अन्यः पुरुष इत्येवंविधस्य विवेकस्य ख्याति॥ प्रख्या सा हानस्य दृश्यपरित्यागस्योपायः कारणं। कीदृशी। अविप्लव। न विद्यते विप्लवो विच्छेदोऽन्तरान्तरा व्युत्थानरूपो यस्याः सा ऽविप्लवा॥

† इदमत्र तात्पर्यम्। प्रतिपक्षभावनाबलादविद्याप्रविलये विनिवृत्तज्ञातृत्वकर्तृत्वाद्यभिमानाया रजस्तमोमलानभिभूताया बुद्धेरन्तर्मुखाया या चिच्छायासंक्रान्तिः सा विवेकख्यातिरित्युच्यते। तस्याञ्च सततत्वेन प्रवृत्तायां दृश्यस्याधिकारनिवृत्तेर्भवत्येव कैवल्यम्॥

‡ उत्पन्नविवेकख्यातेः पुरुषस्य यादृशी प्रज्ञा भवति तां कथयन् विवेकख्यातेरेव स्वरूपमाह॥

तस्य सप्तधा प्रान्तभूमौ प्रज्ञा ॥ २७ ॥

Discriminative knowledge of what nature.

Aph. 27.—Of that [enlightened soul the perfect knowledge, up to the ground of the limit, is of seven kinds.

a. 'Of that' [soul] in which discriminative knowledge has sprung up; 'the perfect knowledge'—in the shape of the discrimination which it behooves us to understand; 'up to the ground of the limit', i. e., as far as is the extent of all the meditation that has a support [—see B. 1. §17, *j*,—]; is of seven sorts.*

b. Among these [seven], that which consists in liberation from the products [of mind] is of four sorts,—(1) "That which is to be known is known by me;" (2) "There is nothing that ought to be known;" (3) "My 'afflictions' are destroyed,—there is nothing of mine requiring to be destroyed;" (4) "Knowledge has been attained by me, discriminative knowledge has been attained by me;"—and so, by the abandonment of all other impressions, in that state of things, just such perfect knowledge takes place [as is spoken of in the aphorism]. Such perfect knowledge, being pure knowledge the object of which is some product [of mind], is what is called 'liberation from the products.'†

---

* तस्योत्पन्नविवेकज्ञानस्य ज्ञातव्यविवेकरूपा प्रज्ञा। प्रान्तभूमौ सकलसालम्बनसमाधिभूमिपर्यन्तं। सप्तप्रकारा भवति॥

† तत्र कार्यविमुक्तिरूपा चतुःप्रकारा। ज्ञातं मया ज्ञेयं। न ज्ञातव्यं किञ्चिदस्ति। क्षीणा मे क्लेशाः न मे किञ्चित् क्षेतव्यमस्ति। अधिगतं मया ज्ञानं प्राप्ता मया विवेकख्यातिरिति प्रत्ययान्तरपरिहारेण तस्यामवस्थायामीदृश्येव प्रज्ञा

c. 'Liberation from the mind' is of three sorts,—(1) "My mind has done its office [in enabling me to discern the distinction of soul and nature];" (2) "and the Qualities have lost their influence [over me],—like stones that have fallen from a mountain-peak they will not again resume their place; for why should these, when tending towards resolution into their cause, spring up again in the absence of the fundamental reason [for their springing up] which is called 'delusion,' and in the absence of a motive?"—(3) "And my meditation is such as has become one with soul;—such being the case, I exist in my real nature." Such is the threefold 'liberation from mind'.*

d. So then, when there has sprung up such a sevenfold perfect knowledge, reckoning as far as to the limit [where meditation ceases to rest upon an object], we say that soul is *alone*† [*kevala*, or in the desiderated state of *kaivalya*].

e. It has been stated [§26] that discriminative knowledge is

जायते। ईदृशी प्रज्ञा कार्यविषयं निर्मलं ज्ञानं कार्यविमुक्तिरित्युच्यते॥

* चित्तविमुक्तिस्त्रिविधा। चरितार्था मे बुद्धिः। गुणाश्च हृताधिकारा गिरिशिखरनिपतिता इव ग्रावाणः पुनः स्थितिं न यास्यन्ति स्वकारणे प्रलयाभिमुखानां मोहाभिधानमूलकारणाभावान्निष्प्रयोजनत्वाच्चामीषां कुतः प्ररोहः। सात्मीभूतश्च मे समाधिः तस्मिन् सति स्वरूपप्रतिष्ठोऽहमिति। ईदृशी त्रिप्रकारा चित्तविमुक्तिः॥

† तदेवमीदृश्यां सप्तविधप्रान्तभूमिप्रज्ञायामुपजातायां पुरुषः केवल इत्युच्यते॥

E

the cause of the removal of the Conjunction [between soul and nature]; but what is the cause of *that?* To this he replies.*

योगाङ्गानुष्ठानादशुद्धिक्षये ज्ञानदीप्तिराविवेक-
ख्यातेः ॥ २८ ॥

Ascetic practices clear the way to discriminative knowledge.

Aph. 28.—Till there is discriminative knowledge, there is, from the practice of the things subservient to the *Yoga*, an illumination [more or less brilliant] of knowledge [which is operative] in the removal of impurity.

a. The 'things subservient to the *Yoga*' are what will be mentioned [in §29]. 'From the practice' of these, i. e. from the practice of them preceded by a knowledge of them,—'till there is discriminative knowledge,'—that 'illumination of knowledge' which, more or less, as a modification of the pure [or enlightening] principle, is [operative] 'in the removal of impurity'—in the removal of impurity in the shape of the 'afflictions' whose characteristic is their hiding the light of the pure principle of the mind,—until discriminative knowledge [takes place], *that* is the cause of this knowledge [of the distinction between soul and nature];—such is the meaning.†

---

* विवेकख्यातिस्संयोगाभावे हेतुरित्युक्तं । तस्यास्तूत्पत्तौ किन्निमित्तमित्यत आह ॥

† योगाङ्गानि वक्ष्यमाणानि । तेषामनुष्ठानाद् ज्ञानपूर्वकादभ्यासादाविवेकख्यातेरशुद्धिक्षये चित्तसत्त्वस्य प्रकाशावरणलक्षणक्लेशरूपाशुद्धिक्षये या ज्ञानदीप्तिस्तारतम्येन सात्त्विकः परिणामो विवेकख्यातिपर्यन्तस्स तस्याः ख्यातेर्हेतुरित्यर्थः ॥

b. 'From the practice of the things subservient to the *Yoga*,—in the removal of impurity,'—has been said:—what, then, are those 'things subservient to the Yoga'? So he enunciates them.*

यमनियमासनप्राणायामप्रत्याहारधारणाध्यान-
समाधयो ऽष्टावङ्गानि ॥ २९ ॥

The eight subservients of Concentration.

Aph. 29.—The eight things subservient [to Concentration] are (1) forbearance, (2) religious observance, (3) postures, (4) suppression of the breath, (5) restraint, (6) attention, (7) contemplation, and (8) meditation.

b. Some of these, as 'attention,' &c., are immediately subservient, since they are directly conducive to meditation. Some, as 'forbearance,' 'religious observance,' &c., conduce to meditation by means of their eradicating [all] hesitation about things opposed to it, such as killing, &c. Of 'postures,' and the rest [in the list,] the conduciveness is successive, it being, e. g., when one has succeeded in regard to 'posture,' that there is steadiness in 'suppression of breath;'—and so it is to be inferred also in respect of the others [in succession].†

---

* योगाङ्गानुष्ठानादशुद्धिक्षय इत्युक्तं । कानि पुनस्तानि योगाङ्गानीति तेषामुद्देशमाह ॥

† इह कानिचित् समाधेः साक्षादुपकारकत्वेनान्तराण्यङ्गानि यथा धारणादीनि । कानिचित् प्रतिपक्षभूतहिंसादिवितर्कोन्मूलनद्वारेण समाधेरुपकुर्वन्ति यथा यमनियमादयः । तत्रासनादीनामुत्तरोत्तरमुपकारकत्वं यथा सत्यासनजये प्राणायामस्थैर्यं । एवमुत्तरत्रापि न्याय्यम् ॥

b. He describes these in their order.*

अहिंसासत्यास्तेयब्रह्मचर्यापरिग्रहा यमः ॥ ३० ॥

Forbearance what. *Aph.* 30.—'Forbearance' *(yama)* consists of not killing, veracity, not stealing, continence, and not coveting.

a. Among these [—to speak first of the first—], 'killing' is acting for the purpose of removing life; and this is a cause of all evils. The absence of this is what is meant by 'not killing.' Since 'killing' must be abstained from at *all* times, its opposite, 'not killing' is set down first† [in the list].

b. 'Veracity' means conformity, in speech and mind, to fact. Its opposite is falsehood. 'Theft' is the taking away another's property. Its absence is 'not stealing.' Continence' is the subjection of one's members. 'Not coveting' means not desiring for one's self means of enjoyment.‡

c. These five, 'not killing,' &c., which are meant by the word

---

* क्रमेणैषां स्वरूपमाह ॥

† तत्र प्राणवियोगप्रयोजनव्यापारो हिंसा। सा च सर्वानर्थहेतुः। तदभावो ऽहिंसा। हिंसायास्सर्वकालमेव परिहार्यत्वात्प्रथमं तदभावाया अहिंसाया निर्देशः ॥

‡ सत्यं वाङ्मनसयोर्यथार्थत्वं। तदभावो ऽसत्यं। स्तेयं परस्वापहरणं। तदभावो ऽस्तेयं। ब्रह्मचर्यं उपस्थसंयमः। अपरिग्रहो भोगसाधनानामस्वीकरणं ॥

forbearance,' are laid down as things conducive to Concentration.*

d. He states a peculiarity of these.†

एते जातिदेशकालसमयानवच्छिन्नाः सार्वभौम-
महाव्रतम् ॥ ३१ ॥

Honesty independent of circumstances.

Aph. 31.—These, without respect to rank, place, time, or compact, are the universal great duty.

a. 'Rank' means Bráhman-hood, &c. 'Place' means a place of pilgrimage, &c., 'Time' means the fourteenth of the month, or other [date which may affect the meritoriousness or otherwise of this or that otherwise perhaps indifferent act]. 'Compact' means that a Bráhman, for example, is the motive [of our doing or leaving undone]. The aforesaid 'forbearances,' viz. 'not killing,' &c., without respect to these four [considerations], abiding in all places—i. e. [as the moral law written on the heart, in all] understandings,—are what are called 'the great duty.'‡

---

* त एते ऽहिंसादयः पञ्च यमशब्दवाच्या योगाङ्गत्वेन निर्दिष्टा ॥

† एषां विशेषमाह ॥

‡ जातिर्ब्राह्मणत्वादिः । देशस्तीर्थादिः । कालश्चतुर्दश्यादिः । समयो ब्राह्मणप्रयोजनादिः । एतैश्चतुर्भिरनवच्छिन्नाः पूर्वोक्ता अहिंसादयो यमाः सर्वासु क्षिप्तादिषु चित्तभूमिषु भवा महाव्रतमित्युच्यते ॥

b. To explain :—'I will not kill a Bráhman,'—'I will not kill any one at a place of pilgrimage,'—'I will not kill any one on the fourteenth of the month,'—'I will not kill, except for the benefit of a god, a Bráhman, or the like,'—[well, the 'forbearances' must be] without this fourfold qualification,—unqualified, —thus 'I will not kill any one, anywhere, at any time, or for any purpose whatever.' And the same holds in respect of 'truth' and the rest, mutatis mutandis. It is these thus unqualified, and acted upon in their full generality, that are called 'the great duty.'*

c. He states what are 'religious observances' *(niyama)*.†

शौचसन्तोषतपःस्वाध्यायेश्वरप्रणिधानानि नियमाः ॥ ३२ ॥

Religious observances.

Aph. 32.—Religious observances *(niyama)* are (1) purification, (2) contentment (3) austerity, (4) inaudible mutterings, and (5) persevering devotion to the Lord.

a. 'Purification' *(śaucha)* is of two sorts, external, and internal. The external is the cleansing of the body by earth, water,

---

* तद्यथा। ब्राह्मणं न हनिष्यामि तीर्थे कञ्चन न हनिष्यामि चतुर्दश्यां न हनिष्यामि देवब्राह्मणाद्यर्थव्यतिरेकेण न हनिष्यामीत्येवं चतुर्विधावच्छेदव्यतिरेकेण कञ्चित् क्वचित् कदाचित् कस्मिंश्चिदप्यर्थे न हनिष्यामीत्यनवच्छिन्नाः। एवं सत्यादिषु यथायोगं योज्यं। इत्थमनियतीभूताः सामान्येनैव प्रवृत्ताः महाव्रतमित्युच्यते॥

† नियमानाह॥

&c. The internal is the washing away the impurity of the mind by means of benevolence, &c.*

b. 'Contentment' *(santosha)* means contentedness. The rest have been already described. These, viz. 'purification,' and the rest, are what are meant by the term 'religious observances.'†

c. How are these subservient to Concentration? To this he replies.‡

वितर्कबाधने प्रतिपक्षभावनम् ॥ ३३ ॥

How these things are of use.

Aph. 33.—In excluding things questionable, the calling up something opposite [is serviceable].

a. 'Killing,' &c., as opponents of Concentration, are 'things questionable,' because they are doubted about [—it being questionable what real good they can do]. If these are excluded when things opposed to them are called up, then concentration is facilitated. Hence 'forbearance' and 'religious observances' really are subservient to Concentration.§

---

* शौचं द्विविधं बाह्यमाभ्यन्तरञ्च। बाह्यं मृज्जलादिभिः कायप्रक्षालनम्। आन्तरं मैत्र्यादिभिश्चित्तमलप्रक्षालनम्॥

† सन्तोषस्तुष्टिः। शेषाः प्रागेव भूतव्याख्यानाः। एते शौचादयो नियमशब्दवाच्याः॥

‡ कथमेषां योगाङ्गत्वमित्यत आह॥

§ वितर्क्यन्त इति वितर्का योगपरिपन्थिनो हिंसादयः। तेषां प्रतिपक्षभावने सति यदि बाधा भवति तदा योगस्सुकरो भवतीति भवत्येव यमनियमानां योगाङ्गत्वम्॥

b. Now he states, in order, the nature, the divisions, the kind, the cause, and the fruit, of the 'things questionable' *(vitarka)*.*

वितर्का हिंसादयः कृतकारितानुमोदिता लोभक्रोधमोहपूर्वका मृदुमध्याधिमात्रा दुःखाज्ञानानन्तफला इति प्रतिपक्षभावनम्॥ ३४ ॥

Account of objectionable things.

Aph. 34.—The 'things questionable,' killing, &c.; whether done, caused to be done, or approved of; whether resulting from covetousness, anger, or delusion; whether slight, of intermediate character, or beyond measure; have no end of fruits [in the shape of] pain and ignorance;—hence the calling up of something opposite [is every way advisable].

a. These the 'killing,' &c., aforesaid are first divided tripartitely through the difference of 'done,' 'caused to be done,' and 'approved of.' Among these, those are 'done,' which are carried into effect by one's self. Those are 'caused to be done,' which are brought about by the employment of the incentive expression 'Do it, do it.' Those are 'approved,' which, when being done by another, are consented to by the expression 'Well done, well done.' And this threefold character is mentioned in order to debar hallucination in regard to these respectively; otherwise some dull-witted one might reflect thus, "The killing was not done by me myself, therefore the blame is not mine."†

---

* इदानीं वितर्काणां स्वरूपं भेदं प्रकारं कारणं फलञ्च क्रमेणाह॥

† एते पूर्वोक्ता हिंसादयः प्रथमं त्रिधा भिद्यन्ते कृतकारितानुमोदितभेदेन। तत्र स्वयं निष्पादिताः कृताः। कुरु-कुर्विति प्रयोजकव्यापारेण समुत्पादिताः कारिताः। अन्येन

b. In order to declare the causes of these ['questionable things'], he says, 'resulting from covetousness, anger, or delusion.'*

c. Although 'covetousness' is the one first specified, yet, since the source of *all* the 'afflictions' is delusion, whose mark is the conceit that what is *not* soul is soul, *this* we must be sure is the root, because, when *it* takes place, 'covetousness' 'anger' and the rest arise in consequence of there having gone before the division of *self* and *other one* [—but for the existence of which delusive division there would have been no room for either covetousness or anger]. We mean, then, that every class of evils results from delusion.†

d. 'Covetousness' is a thirst. 'Anger' is an inflamed condition of the mind, which uproots all discrimination between what ought to be done and what ought not to be done.‡

क्रियमाणाः साधु साध्वित्यङ्गीकृता अनुमोदिताः। एतच्च त्रैविध्यं परस्परव्यामोहनिवारणायोच्यते। अन्यथा मन्दमतिरेवं मन्येत न मया स्वयं हिंसा कृतेति नास्ति मे दोष इति।

* एतेषां कारणप्रतिपादनायाह लोभक्रोधमोहपूर्वका इति ॥

† यद्यपि लोभः प्रथमं निर्दिष्टस्तथापि सर्वक्लेशानां मोहस्यानात्मन्यात्माभिमानलक्षणस्य निदानत्वात् तस्मिन् सति स्वपरविभागपूर्वकत्वेन लोभक्रोधादीनामुद्भवान्मूलत्वमवसेयं। मोहपूर्विका सर्वा दोषजातिरित्यर्थः ॥

‡ लोभस्तृष्णा। क्रोधः कृत्याकृत्यविवेकोन्मूलकः प्रज्वलनात्मकश्चित्तधर्मः ॥

F

e. 'Killing,' &c., moreover, which are severally threefold through the distinction between 'done,' &c., [§34. *a.*], are divided tripartitely through their having as their cause 'delusion,' &c., [§34. *b*]. He mentions, of these again, a threefold character, through their difference of state, as 'slight, of intermediate character, and beyond measure.' The 'slight,' or slow, are those that are neither fierce nor middling. Those 'of intermediate character,' are what are neither slow nor fierce. Those that are 'beyond measure' are what are vehement, neither middling nor slight. Thus the nine divisions, since there is thus a further threefold character, become twenty-seven.*

f. The 'slight,' &c., moreover severally may be of three sorts through the distinction of slight, intermediate, and excessive. These are to be combined accordingly as they can combine. For example, the 'slightly slight,' the 'slightly intermediate,' the 'slightly excessive,' and so on.†

g. He mentions their fruit, saying, 'having no end of fruits [in the shape of] pain and ignorance.' 'Pain' is a state of mind, dependent on the Quality of passion, exhibiting itself as some-

---

* प्रत्येकं कृतादिभेदेन त्रिप्रकारा अपि हिंसादयो मोहादिकारणत्वेन त्रिधा भिद्यन्ते। तेषामेव पुनरवस्थाभेदेन त्रैविध्यमाह मृदुमध्याधिमात्राः। . मृदवो मन्दा न तीव्रा नापि मध्यमाः। मध्या न मन्दा नापि तीव्राः। अधिमात्राः तीव्रा न मध्या नापि मन्दा इति नव भेदा इत्थं त्रैविध्ये सति सप्तविंशतिः॥

† मृद्वादीनामपि प्रत्येकं मृदुमध्याधिमात्रभेदात् त्रैविध्यं सम्भवति। तद्यथायोगं योज्यं। तद्यथा। मृदुमृदुमृदुमध्यौ मृदुतीव्र इत्यादि॥

thing repugnant. 'Ignorance' is false knowledge, in the shape of doubt or error. Those ['questionable things'] of which the endless, or unlimited, fruits are these two, viz. pain and ignorance, are what are so spoken of* [—i. e. spoken of by the compound epithet here analysed].

h. Thus it is enjoined, that the Yogi, by meditating on 'something opposite' is to get rid of these ['questionable things'] which he has understood by means of the division of natures, causes, &c.,† [that has been now set forth].

i. With a view to declare, in order, how perfections arise, consequent on these ['forbearances,' &c.], when, by practice, they have reached their highest degree, he says.‡—

तत्सन्निधौ वैरत्यागः ॥ ३५ ॥

Influence of the Yogi that is harmless.

Aph. 35.—When harmlessness is complete, near him, there is abandonment of enmity.

a. When the harmlessness of him that practises harmlessness is complete, even natural enemies, as the snake and the mungoose, abandon [when near him] their enmity, and abide in amity;—

* एषां फलमाह दुःखाज्ञानान्तफला इति। दुःखं प्रतिकूलतयावभासमानो राजसश्चित्तधर्मः। अज्ञानं मिथ्याज्ञानं संशयविपर्ययरूपं। ते दुःखाज्ञाने अनन्तमपरिच्छिन्नं फलं येषां ते तथोक्ताः ॥

† इत्थं तेषां स्वरूपकारणादिभेदेन ज्ञातानां प्रतिपक्षभावनया योगिना परिहारः कर्त्तव्य इत्युपदिष्टम्भवति ॥

‡ एषामभ्यासात् प्रकर्षमागच्छतामनु निष्पादिन्यः सिद्धयो यथा भवन्ति तथा क्रमेण प्रतिपादयितुमाह ।

that is to say, those that delight in destroying, leave off their destructiveness.*

b. What happens in respect of him that practises veracity? To this he replies.†

सत्यप्रतिष्ठायां क्रियाफलाश्रयत्वम्॥ ३३॥

Influence of veracity. *Aph.* 36.—When veracity is complete, he is the receptacle of the fruit of works.

a. For works, such as sacrifices, being performed, give fruits, such as Paradise. But of that Yogi who practises veracity, the veracity rises to such a degree that the Yogi receives the fruit even without the work's being performed. At his bidding, the fruit of works accrues to any one soever, even though not performing the work:—such is the meaning.‡

b. He states the fruit accruing to him that practises abstinence from theft.§

---

* तस्याहिंसां भावयतोऽहिंसाप्रतिष्ठायां सहजविरोधिनामप्यहिनकुलादीनां वैरत्यागो निर्मत्सरतयावस्थानं भवति। हिंसारताः हिंस्रत्वं परित्यजन्तीत्यर्थः॥

† सत्याभ्यासवतः किं भवतीत्याह॥

‡ क्रियमाणा हि क्रिया यागादिकाः फलं स्वर्गादिकं प्रयच्छन्ति। तस्य तु सत्याभ्यासवतो योगिनस्तथा सत्यं प्रकृष्यते यथा अकृतायामपि क्रियायां योगी फलमाप्नोति। तद्वचनाद्यस्य कस्यचित् क्रियामकुर्वतोऽपि क्रियाफलं भवतीत्यर्थः॥

§ अस्तेयाभ्यासवतः फलमाह॥

अस्तेयप्रतिष्ठायां सर्वरत्नोपस्थानम् ॥ ३७ ॥

The reward of not thieving.

Aph. 37.—When abstinence from theft is complete, all jewels come near him.

a. When he practises abstinence from theft, then, on its reaching its highest degree, the jewels that exist in every quarter come to him even though he covet them not.*

b. He states the fruit of the practice of continence.†

ब्रह्मचर्यप्रतिष्ठायां वीर्यलाभः ॥ ३८ ॥

The reward of continence.

Aph. 38.—When continence is complete, there is gain of strength.

a. He, indeed, that practises continence, when it is complete, there is revealed in him excessive strength, or power. For continence is the preserving of one's manly vigour; and from this [continence] being of a high degree, vigour in body, organs, and mind, attains a high degree.‡

b. He states the fruit of the practice of non-covetousness.§

---

* अस्तेयं यदाभ्यस्यति तदा तस्य प्रकर्षान्निरभिलाषस्यापि सर्वतो दिक्स्थानि रत्नान्युपतिष्ठन्ते ॥

† ब्रह्मचर्याभ्यासस्य फलमाह ॥

‡ यः किल ब्रह्मचर्यमभ्यस्यति तस्य तत्प्रकर्षान्निरतिशयं वीर्यं सामर्थ्यमाविर्भवति । वीर्यनिरोधो हि ब्रह्मचर्यं तस्य प्रकर्षाच्छरीरेन्द्रियमनःसु वीर्यं प्रकर्षमागच्छति ॥

§ अपरिग्रहाभ्यासस्य फलमाह ॥

अपरिग्रहस्थैर्ये जन्मकथन्तासम्बोधः ॥ ३९ ॥

The reward of non-covetousness.

Aph. 39.—When non covetousness is established, there is knowledge of all about [former] states of existence.

a. 'All about it' means the condition how [—*kathantá* being the abstract of the indeclinable *katham*]. 'All about states of existence,' such is the meaning of *janma-kathantá*. The 'knowledge' thereof, the perfect understanding. That is to say, he knows perfectly every thing in regard to the question 'Who was I in a former state of existence? What sort of person? The doer of what actions?'*

b. It is not merely the coveting of the means of enjoyment that is [here meant by] covetousness. Covetousness is [meant] even as far as the soul's coveting a body. Since a body is an instrument of enjoyment whilst *it* exists, from its association with desires, our energy being directed to the external, no real knowledge reveals itself. When, again, without regard to coveting a body, &c., one betakes one's self to indifference, then, since one abandons desire, &c., the acquaintance with past and future states of existence becomes indeed a cause of right knowledge to the indifferent† [person, who thus discerns how little there is deserving of a wise man's regard in any mundane condition whatever].

---

* कथमित्यस्य भावः कथन्ता । जन्मनः कथन्ता जन्मकथन्ता । तस्याः सम्बोधः सम्यक् ज्ञानं । जन्मान्तरे कोऽहमासं कीदृशः किङ्कार्यकारीति जिज्ञासायां सर्वमेव सम्यक् जानातीत्यर्थः ॥

† न केवलं भोगसाधनपरिग्रह एव परिग्रहः । यावदात्मनः शरीरपरिग्रहोऽपि परिग्रहः । भोगसाधनत्वाच्छरी-

c. The fruits of the 'forbearances' have been stated. Now he mentions [those of] the 'religious observances.'*

शौचात्स्वाङ्गजुगुप्सा परैरसंसर्गः॥ ४०।

Mental result of purifications.

Aph. 40.—From 'purification,' loathing for one's own members, and non-intercourse with others.

a. He who practises 'purification,' to him there springs up a loathing, an aversion, even for his own members, through his thoroughly discerning the cause and nature [of a body];—"This body is impure; any fondness for it is not to be entertained;"—and so for the same reason, there is 'non-intercourse,' the absence of intercourse, the avoidance of intercourse, 'with others,' with other possessors also of bodies;—such is the meaning. For whoso loathes his own body, through his discernment of this or that fault, how must he judge of intercourse with the similar bodies of others?†

रस्य तस्मिन् सति रागानुबन्धाद्बहिर्मुखायामेव प्रवृत्तौ न तात्त्विकज्ञानप्रादुर्भावः। यदा पुनः शरीरादिपरिग्रहनैरपेक्ष्येण माध्यस्थ्यमवलम्बते तदा मध्यस्थस्य रागादित्यागात्सम्यग्ज्ञानहेतुर्भवत्येव पूर्वापरजन्मसम्बोधः॥

* उक्ता यमानां सिद्धयः। अथ नियमानाह।

† यः शौचं भावयति तस्य स्वाङ्गेष्वपि कारणस्वरूपपर्यालोचनद्वारेण जुगुप्सा घृणा समुपजायते अशुचिरयं कायो नात्राग्रहः कर्त्तव्य इत्यमुनैव हेतुना परैरन्यैश्च कायवद्भिरसंसर्गः संसर्गाभावः संसर्गपरिवर्ज्जनमित्यर्थः। यः किल स्वमेव

b. He states another fruit of this same 'purification.'*

सत्त्वशुद्धिसौमनस्यैकाग्र्येन्द्रियजयात्मदर्शनयोग्य-
त्वानि च ॥ ४१ ॥

Other results of purifications.

Aph. 41.—And purity in the Quality of Goodness, complacency, intentness, subjugation of the senses, and fitness for the beholding of soul, [are fruits of 'purification'].

a. 'Are' is required to complete the sentence.†

b. The 'Quality of goodness' is what consists of light, joy, &c., [—see Sánkhya Aphorisms B. I. §62]; its 'purity' is its not being oppressed by Passion and Darkness. 'Complacency' is mental joy, from there not being the oppression of distress. 'Intentness' is steadiness of the mind on an object to which the senses are confined. 'Subjugation of the senses' is the abiding in themselves of the senses averted from objects. The 'fitness' of the mind means its power of beholding soul,—[this 'beholding' being] in the shape of the knowledge of the distinctness‡ [of soul from Nature].

कायं जुगुप्सते तत्तद्वद्यदर्शनात्कथं परकीयैस्तथाभूतैः कायैः संसर्गमनुभवति ॥

* शौचस्यैव फलान्तरमाह ॥

† भवन्तीति वाक्यशेषः ॥

‡ सत्त्वं प्रकाशसुखाद्यात्मकं। तस्य शुद्धिः रजस्तमोभ्यामनभिभवः। सौमनस्यं खेदाननुभवेन मानसी प्रीतिः। एकाग्रता नियतेन्द्रियविषये चेतसः स्थैर्यं। इन्द्रियजयो विषयपराङ्मुखानामिन्द्रियाणां स्वात्मन्यवस्थानं। आत्मदर्शने विवेकख्यातिरूपे चित्तस्य योग्यत्वं समर्थत्वं ॥

c. These, 'purity in the Quality of Goodness,' and the rest, manifest themselves in succession, in the case of him that practises purifications. That is to say, from 'purification' comes 'purity in the Quality of Goodness;' from 'purity in the Quality of Goodness,' 'complacency; from 'complacency,' intentness; from 'intentness,' 'subjugation of the senses;' and from 'subjugation of the senses,' 'fitness for the beholding of soul.'*

d. He states the fruit of the practice of contentment.†

सन्तोषादनुत्तमसुखलाभः ॥ ४२ ॥

The fruit of contentment.

Aph. 42.—From contentment there is acquired superlative felicity.

a. From contentment's reaching its highest degree, there is revealed to the Yogi such an inward joy that the external enjoyment of objects is not equal to a hundreth part of it.‡

b. He states the fruit of 'austerity' *(tapas)*.§

कायेन्द्रियसिद्धिरशुद्धिक्षयात्तपसः ॥ ४३ ॥

---

* शौचाभ्यासवत एते सत्त्वशुद्ध्यादयः क्रमेण प्रादुर्भवन्ति। शौचात् सत्त्वशुद्धिः। सत्त्वशुद्धेः सौमनस्यं। सौमनस्यादैकाग्र्यं। ऐकाग्र्यादिन्द्रियजयः। इन्द्रियजयादात्मदर्शनयोग्यतेति॥

† सन्तोषाभ्यासस्य फलमाह॥

‡ सन्तोषप्रकर्षेण योगिनस्तथाविधमान्तरं सुखमाविर्भवति यस्य बाह्यं विषयसुखं शतांशेनापि न समम्॥

§ तपसः फलमाह॥

G

The fruit of austerity.

Aph. 43.—The perfection of the bodily senses, by the removal of impurity, [is the fruit] of austerity.

a. 'Austerity,' when thoroughly practised, brings 'perfection,' i. e. a heightening, of the bodily senses, through the removal of the impurity, consisting in the 'afflictions,' &c., of the mind.*

b. What is meant is this;—by the *chándráyaṇa* [species of fast], and the like, there is the removal of the 'afflictions' [§ 3] of the mind. By the removal of these there is developed, in the senses, the power of, for example, discerning the subtile, the hidden, and the infinite; and, in the body, [the power of assuming] at will either an atomic or an enormous bulk, &c.†

c. He states the fruit of 'inaudible muttering' *swádhyáya*.‡

स्वाध्यायादिष्टदेवतासम्प्रयोगः ॥ ४४ ॥

The fruit of inaudible muttering.

Aph. 44.—Through inaudible muttering there is a meeting with one's favourite deity.

a. When 'inaudible muttering,' in the shape of charms and spells directed [to some deity or other], is at its height, there

---

* तपः समभ्यस्यमानं चेतसः क्लेशादिलक्षणाशुद्धिक्षयद्वारेण कायेन्द्रियाणां सिद्धिमुत्कर्षमादधाति ॥

† अयमर्थः। चान्द्रायणादिना चित्तक्लेशक्षयः। तत्क्षयादिन्द्रियाणां सूक्ष्मव्यवहितविप्रकृष्टदर्शनादिसामर्थ्यमाविर्भवति कायस्य यथेच्छमणुमहत्त्वादीनि ॥

‡ स्वाध्यायस्य फलमाह ॥

takes place, in the case of the Yogi, a meeting with the 'favourite' deity, i. e. with the one to whom this [inaudible muttering] was directed. That is to say, the deity becomes visible* [—and most probably says "Ask a boon"].

b. He states the fruit of 'persevering devotion to the Lord' (*íswara-pranidhána*).†

समाधिसिद्धिरीश्वरप्रणिधानात्॥ ४५ ॥

The fruit of persevering devotion to the Lord.

Aph. 45.—Perfection in meditation comes from persevering devotion to the Lord.

a. As for this species of faith in the Lord, there is developed therefrom Meditation, which has been already described,—because that Divine Lord, being pleased, having removed the obstructive 'afflictions,' elicits meditation.‡

b. Having spoken of the 'forbearances' and the 'religious observances' [§29], he speaks of the 'postures' (*ásana*).§

---

* अभिप्रेतमन्त्रजपादिलक्षणे स्वाध्याये प्रकृष्यमाणे योगिन इष्टया अभिप्रेतया देवतया सम्प्रयोगो भवति। सा देवता प्रत्यक्षीभवतीत्यर्थः॥

† ईश्वरप्रणिधानस्य फलमाह॥

‡ ईश्वरे यो ऽयं भक्तिविशेषः तस्मात्समाधेरुक्तलक्षणस्याविर्भावो भवति यस्मात्स भगवानीश्वरः प्रसन्नः सन्नन्तरायरूपान् क्लेशानपहृत्य समाधिमुद्बोधयति॥

§ यमनियमानुक्त्वासनमाह॥

स्थिरसुखमासनम् ॥ ४६ ॥

Postures what.

Aph. 46.—A 'posture' is what is steady and pleasant.

a. A 'posture' means what one sets one's self in,—such as the *padma*, the *daṇḍa*, the *swastika*, &c., [with the precise character of which we are not at present concerned]. When this is 'steady,'—not wavering,—and 'pleasant,'—not uncomfortable,—then this serves as a subservient to Concentration.*

b. He mentions a plan for producing steadiness and pleasantness in this same.†

प्रयत्नशैथिल्यानन्त्यसमापत्तिभ्याम् ॥ ४७ ॥

'Postures' how managed.

Aph. 47.—Through slightness of effort and through attaining to the infinite [do 'postures,' become steady and pleasant].

a. The construction [with the preceding aphorisms] is this, that that,—viz., 'posture,' becomes steady and pleasant through slightness of effort and through attaining to the infinite.‡

---

* आस्यते अनेनेत्यासनं। पद्मासनदण्डासनस्वस्तिकासनादि। तद्यदा स्थिरं निष्कम्पं सुखं अनुद्वेजनीयं भवति तदा तद्योगाङ्गतां भजते ॥

† तस्यैव स्थिरसुखत्वापत्त्यर्थमुपायमाह ॥

‡ तदासनं प्रयत्नशैथिल्येनानन्त्यसमापत्त्या च स्थिरं सुखं भवतीति सम्बन्धः ॥

b. When, when he forms the wish—"Let me establish [myself in such and such] a posture,"—that 'posture' is effected with slight effort, with little trouble; and when the mind attains to the boundlessness that belongs to space,—i. e. when in thought one has identified one's self with it,—then, from there being neither body nor self-consciousness, the 'posture' is no cause of pain;—when *this* command over the 'postures' has been attained, the tremblings, &c. [B. I. §31], which are obstacles to meditation, no longer prevail.*

c. He mentions a fruit of this same when accomplished.†

ततो द्वन्द्वानभिघातः ॥ ४८ ॥

Fruit of the 'postures.'

Aph. 48.—Thence there is no assault by the pairs.

a. When this command of the 'postures' has been attained, the Yogi is not assailed by 'the pairs,' cold and heat, hunger and thirst, &c.;—such is the meaning.‡

---

* यदा यदासनं बध्नामीति इच्छां करोति प्रयत्नशैथिल्ये ऽप्यक्लेशेनैव तदासनं निष्पद्यते। यदा आकाशगते आनन्त्ये चेतसः समापत्तिः क्रियते अवधानेन तादात्म्यमापद्यते तदा देहाहङ्काराभावान्नासनं दुःखजनकं भवति। अस्मिंश्चासनजये सति समाध्यन्तरायभूता न प्रभवन्त्यङ्गमेजयत्वादयः॥

† तस्यैवानुनिष्पादितस्य फलमाह॥

‡ तस्मिन्नासनजये सति द्वन्द्वैः शीतोष्णक्षुत्तृष्णादिभिर्योगी नाभिहन्यत इत्यर्थः॥

b. Next after the mastering of the 'postures,' he speaks of the 'regulation of the breath' *(práṇáyáma)*.*

तस्मिन् सति श्वासप्रश्वासयोर्गतिविच्छेदः प्राणा-
यामः ॥ ४९ ॥

Regulation of the breath.

Aph. 49.—When this has taken place, there is regulation of the breath, a cutting short of the motion of inspiration and expiration.

a. When steadiness in a 'posture' has taken place, that species of auxiliary of Concentration, viz., 'regulation of the breath,' to which this [steadiness of posture] is conducive, is to be practised. Of what sort is this? In the shape of 'a cutting short of the motion of inspiration and expiration'.†

b. 'Inspiration and expiration' are what have been described [B. I. §31, *e*]. What is called 'regulation of the breath,' is the 'cutting short,' or restraining, 'of the motion,' or flow, in the places external or internal [—see §51—], of these two by means of the threefold process of [regulated] expiration, retention, and inspiration,‡[—see B. I. §34, *a*].

---

* आसनजयादनन्तरं प्राणायाममाह ॥

† आसनस्थैर्ये सति तन्निमित्तकः प्राणायामलक्षणो योगाङ्गविशेषोऽनुष्ठेयो भवति । कीदृशः । श्वासप्रश्वासयोर्गतिविच्छेदलक्षणः ॥

‡ श्वासप्रश्वासौ कृतलक्षणौ । तयोस्त्रिधा रेचनकुम्भनपूरणद्वारेण वाह्याभ्यन्तरेषु स्थानेषु गतेः प्रवाहस्य विच्छेदो धारणं प्राणायाम उच्यते ॥

c. In order that this same may be easily understood, he states the nature of it, with its divisions.*

स तु वाह्याभ्यन्तरस्तम्भवृत्तिर्देशकालसंख्याभिः परिदृष्टो दीर्घसूक्ष्मः ॥ ५० ॥

This explained. *Aph.* 50.—But this, which is (1) outer, (2) inner, and (3) steady, peculiarised by place, time, and number, is long or short.

a. 'That which is outer' is the expiration, or expelling; 'that which is inner' is the inspiration, or filling; 'that which abides steady,' within, is called *kumbhaka.* It is called *kumbhaka* because, when it takes place, the vital spirits rest motionless like water in a jar (*kumbha*).†

b. This threefold regulation of the breath, further peculiarised by place, time, and number, is termed 'long or short'. 'Peculiarised by place,' e. g., [see the direction] "As regards beginning and end, twelve from the nose;"—that is to say, as far as twelve inches, beginning from the nose. 'Peculiarised by time,' as, "For the duration of thirty six *mátras,*" &c. Peculiarised by number,'—e. g. the first *udváta* is made by so many inspirations and expirations, so many times; and the employment of number is had recourse to in order that this may be known [by substituting the definite number for the indefinite 'so many']. By *udváta* is meant the impinging of the air sent [upwards, in speak-

* तस्यैव सुखावगमाय विभज्य स्वरूपं कथयति ॥

† वाह्यवृत्तिः श्वासो रेचकः । अन्तर्वृत्तिः प्रश्वासः पूरकः । अन्तस्तम्भवृत्तिः कुम्भकः । तस्मिन् जलमिव कुम्भे निश्चलतया प्राणा अवस्थाप्यन्ते इति कुम्भकः ॥

ing,] from the pit of the stomach, on the head,* [from which it is supposed to be reflected down again, so passing out of the mouth].

b. Having mentioned three regulations of the breath, in order to declare a fourth one, he says.†

बाह्याभ्यन्तरविषयाक्षेपी चतुर्थः ॥ ५१ ॥

A special variety.

Aph. 51.—The fourth recognises both the outer and the inner spheres.

a. The 'outer sphere' of the breath is that [space] from beginning to end [—reckoning from the nose—] of twelve [inches;—see §50, *b*]. The 'inner sphere' is the heart, the navel, the plexus, &c. The fourth regulation of the breath is that which, in the shape of motionlessness, is a cutting off of the motion [of the breath], recognising, i. e. having an eye upon, both those two spheres.‡

---

* त्रिविधोऽयं प्राणायामो देशेन कालेन संख्यया चोपलक्षितो दीर्घसूक्ष्मसंज्ञको भवति। देशेनोपलक्षितो यथा नासाद्द्वादशान्तादौ नासामारभ्य द्वादशाङ्गुलपर्यन्तमित्यर्थः। कालेनोपलक्षितो यथा षट्त्रिंशन्मात्रादिप्रमाणः। संख्ययोपलक्षितो यथा इयतो वारान् कृत एतावद्भिः श्वासप्रश्वासैः प्रथम उद्घातो भवति एतज्ज्ञानाय संख्याग्रहणमुपात्तं। उद्घातो नाभिमूलात्प्रेरितस्य वायोः शिरस्यभिहननम्॥

† त्रीन् प्राणायामानभिधाय चतुर्थमभिधातुमाह॥

‡ प्राणस्य बाह्यो विषयो द्वादशान्तादिः। अन्तरो

b. The distinction between this and the third one, viz., the *kumbhaka* [§50, *a*,] is this. That one [—the *kumbhaka*—], without paying any regard to the two spheres, the outer and the inner, suddenly, like a lotus dropped upon a heated stone, at once arrives at the condition of rigidity;—but *this* one is a restrainment that has respect to the two spheres.*

c. This also, like the former [§50, *b*], is to be regarded as being peculiarised by time, space, and number.†

d. Of this [regulation of the breath] which is of four descriptions, he mentions the fruit.‡

ततः क्षीयते प्रकाशावरणम् ॥ ५२ ॥

The fruit of the regulation of the breath.

Aph. 52.—Thereby is removed the obscuration of the light.

a. 'Thereby,' i. e. by that regulation of the breath, there is 'removed,' or destroyed, that 'obscuration' which, in the shape

---

विषयो हृदयनाभिचक्रादिः तौ द्वौ विषयावाक्षिप्य पर्यालोच्य यो विष्टम्भरूपो गतिविच्छेदः स चतुर्थः प्राणायामः ॥

* तृतीयस्मात्कुम्भकादयमस्य विशेषः । स बाह्याभ्यन्तरौ विषयावपर्यालोच्यैव सहसा तप्तोपलनिपतितजलजन्यायेन युगपत् स्तम्भवृत्त्या निष्पद्यते । अस्य तु विषयद्वयाक्षेपको निरोधः ॥

† अयमपि पूर्ववद्देशकालसंख्याभिरुपलक्षितो द्रष्टव्यः ॥

‡ चतुर्विधस्यास्य फलमाह ॥

H

of the 'afflictions' [§3], there is 'of the light,' that belongs to the Pure Quality of the mind;—such is the meaning.*

b. He mentions another result.†

धारणासु च योग्यता मनसः ॥ ५३ ॥

A further result.

Aph. 53.—And the mind becomes fit for acts of attention.

a. 'Acts of attention' are what will be spoken of [in the sequel]. The mind, freed from its defects by the several kinds of regulation of the breath, wherever it is directed to, there it remains fixed, and does not suffer distraction.‡

b. He defines 'restraint' *(pratyáhára)*.§

स्वस्वविषयसम्प्रयोगाभावे चित्तस्य स्वरूपानुकार इवेन्द्रियाणां प्रत्याहारः ॥ ५४ ॥

'Restraint' what.

Aph. 54.—'Restraint' is as it were the accommodation of the senses to the nature of the mind in the absence of concernment with each one's own object.

---

* ततः तस्मात्प्राणायामात् प्रकाशस्य चित्तसत्त्वगतस्य यदावरणं क्लेशरूपं तत् क्षीयते विनश्यतीत्यर्थः ॥

† फलान्तरमाह ॥

‡ धारणा वक्ष्यमाणाः । तासु प्राणायामैः क्षीणदोषं मनो यत्र यत्र धार्यते तत्र तत्र स्थिरं भवति न विक्षेपं भजते ॥

§ प्रत्याहारस्य लक्षणमाह ॥

a. It is called 'restraint,' because, when it exists, the senses are restrained, are withheld, from their respective objects. And how is this effected? He replies;—'of the senses,' Sight, &c., there is 'each one's own object,' as Colour, &c:—'concernment' therewith is any energizing with respect thereto:—the 'absence' of this is the abiding in their mere nature after having abandoned all regard to such things. When this takes place, the senses simply accommodate themselves to the nature of the mind; for, all the senses are observed to follow obsequiously the mind, as the bees their leader. Hence, when the mind is restrained [from the exercise of its functions], these [senses] are restrained; and their accommodation to the nature thereof [under such circumstances] is what is called 'restraint'.*

b. He states the fruit.†

ततः परमा वश्यतेन्द्रियाणाम् ॥ ५५ ॥

The fruit of restraint. *Aph.* 55.—Therefrom is there complete subjection of the senses.

---

* इन्द्रियाणि स्वस्वविषयेभ्यः प्रत्याह्रीयन्ते प्रतिकूलतया ह्रीयन्ते ऽस्मिन्निति प्रत्याहारः। स च कथं निष्पद्यत इत्याह। चक्षुरादीनामिन्द्रियाणां स्वः स्वो विषयो रूपादिः। तेन सम्प्रयोगस्तदाभिमुख्येन प्रवर्त्तनं। तदभावस्तदाभिमुख्यं परित्यज्य स्वरूपमात्रे ऽवस्थानं। तस्मिन् सति चित्तस्वरूपमात्रानुकारीणीन्द्रियाणि भवन्ति यतश्चित्तमनुवर्त्तमानानि मधुकरराजमिव मधुकरमक्षिकाः सर्वाणीन्द्रियाणि प्रतीयन्ते। अतश्चित्तनिरोधे तानि प्रत्याहृतानि भवन्ति। तेषां तत्स्वरूपानुकारः प्रत्याहार उक्तः॥

† फलमाह॥

a. For, when 'restraint' is practised, the senses become so subjected, so subdued, that, even when attracted towards external objects, they will not go;—such is the meaning.*

Recapitulation. *b*. Thus, then, [—to recapitulate briefly—] of Concentration, which was defined in the First Book, having declared that appendage, viz., the 'Practical [part of] Concentration' [§1], the fruit of which is the alleviating of of the 'afflictions' [§2]; having mentioned the names of the 'afflictions' [§3], their cause and source [§4], their nature and fruit [§5—11]; having stated also the division, cause, nature, and fruit, of works [§12]; the nature and cause of fructification are set forth [§13—14]. Then, since the 'afflictions,' &c., are to be got rid of, and since it is impossible to get rid of them without knowing what they are, and since knowledge is dependant on instruction, and since the instruction assumes four aspects, as it respects (1) what is to be got rid of, (2) what is not [desired] to be got rid of, (3) what is constituted by the cause, and (4) what is the cause constitutive, and since, without [an explanation of what is meant by the expression] 'getting rid of,' the nature of 'what is to be got rid of' cannot be explained, [therefore] having set forth the fourfold arrangement, with [an explanation of what is meant by] 'getting rid of', and with [an account of] the cause of each thing severally [§15—27]; having explained, along with the fruits, the nature of those appliances, 'forbearance,' &c., which stand in the relation of causes, immediate or mediate, in respect of the constitutive cause [of emancipation], viz., 'discriminative knowledge' [§28—46]; having exhibited the 'postures,' &c., as far as 'attention,' arranged according to their mutual relation as conduced to and conducers [§47—52]; their fruits,

* अभ्यस्यमाने हि प्रत्याहारे तथा वश्यान्यायत्तानीन्द्रियाणि सम्पद्यन्ते यथा बाह्यविषयाभिमुखतां नीयमानान्यपि न यान्तीत्यर्थः ।

along with the respective characters thereof, have been set forth [§53—55].*

c. Thus this 'Concentration,' having, through 'forbearance,' 'religious observances,' &c., attained to the condition of a seed, and having sprouted by means of the 'postures' and 'regulation of the breath,' and having blossomed by means of 'self-restraint,' will fructify by means of 'attention,' 'contemplation,' and 'meditation' [§29]. Thus has the Book on the Means been explained.†

---

* तदेवं प्रथमपादोक्तलक्षणस्य योगस्याङ्गभूतं क्लेशतनूकरणफलं क्रियायोगमभिधाय क्लेशानामुद्देशं कारणं क्षेत्रं स्वरूपं फलं चोक्त्वा कर्म्मणामपि भेदं कारणं स्वरूपं फलं चाभिधाय विपाकस्य स्वरूपं कारणं चाभिहितम् ततस्त्याज्यत्वात्क्लेशादीनां ज्ञानव्यतिरेकेण त्यागस्याशक्यत्वात् ज्ञानस्य च शास्त्रायत्तत्वात् शास्त्रस्य च हेयाहेयकारणोपादेयोपादानकारणत्वेन चतुर्व्यूहत्वाद्धेयस्य हानव्यतिरेकेण स्वरूपानिष्पत्तेर्हानसहितं चतुर्व्यूहं स्वस्वकारणसहितमभिधाय उपादानकारणभूताया विवेकख्यातेः कारणभूतानामन्तरङ्गबहिरङ्गभावेन स्थितानां योगानां यमादीनां स्वरूपं फलसहितं व्याकृत्य धारणापर्यन्तानां चासनादीनां परस्परमुपकार्य्योपकारकभावेनावस्थितानामुद्देशमभिधाय परस्परलक्षणपूर्वकं फलमभिहितम्॥

† तदयं योगो यमनियमादिभिः प्राप्तबीजभावः आसनप्राणायामैरङ्कुरितः प्रत्याहारेण कुसुमितो धारणाध्यानसमाधिभिः फलिष्यतीति व्याख्यातः साधनपादः॥

d. Thus has been completed the Second Book—that on the Means—of the commentary called the *Rája Mártanḍa*, composed by the illustrious great king and governor, king Bhojarájá, on the Aphorisms of Patanjali's System of the Yoga.*

---

* इति श्री राजाधिराजभोजदेवविरचितायां राजमार्तण्डाभिधायां पातञ्जलयोगशास्त्रसूत्रवृत्तौ द्वितीयः साधनपादः समाप्तः ॥

END OF BOOK II.